Three Legs
in the
Irish Sea

Tree Cassyn
ayns
Mooir Vannin

Trevor Barrett
Photography by Simon Park

© 2008 Lily Publications
PO Box 33, Ramsey
Isle of Man IM99 4LP

Tel: +44 (0)1624 898446
Fax: +44 (0)1624 898449

E-mail: info@lilypublications.co.uk
Web: www.lilypublications.co.uk

Contents

4. FOREWORD   *A few lines from Manx Telecom*

8. ONE   *We do like to be beside the seaside*

24. TWO   *Mind your language*

38. THREE   *Across the sea and over the hills*

52. FOUR   *Three recurring*

68. FIVE   *Miss Marple investigates*

82. SIX   *Break a leg*

96. SEVEN   *An extraordinary island race*

112. EIGHT   *Creatures real and imagined*

126. NINE   *Man the lifeboats*

142. TEN   *There's no smoke without kippers*

154. ELEVEN   *We do like to do it beside the seaside*

A few lines from Manx Telecom

Manx Telecom always has been, and always will be, in the business of making connections – and not just through the medium of a phone line.

Connecting with the community embraces a mind-boggling variety of uniquely Manx activities: playing in the island's brass bands; giving support to Sailing for the Disabled, the Special Olympics and other local charities; and supporting Manx Language Week and Yn Chruinnaght – a celebration of Isle of Man culture – as well as other annual events and long-running community projects such as the Computer Bus for schools.

One particularly rewarding project, deserving of special mention, was the creation and 2007 opening of Hospice Isle of Man's superb new purpose-built palliative care facilities at Strang. This dream drew everyone together and produced a massive team effort, both in the company and in the community.

Manx Telecom's long list of fundraising events along the way included everything from cake-baking days to retirement and small-change collections to summer ball raffles, raising the grand total of £71,000 – money which helped give the new hospice a state-of-the-art communications system. Many members of Manx Telecom staff also gave generously of their time and expertise in helping the Hospice team with specialist processes and procedures. And through

the mobile phone recycling scheme, the company helped plant around 200 trees in the hospice grounds.

Three Legs in the Irish Sea is all about making connections too – a new book with which Manx Telecom is very pleased to be associated. Alongside the stunning photographs of the Isle of Man's magnificent landscape is a commentary which above all sets out to entertain, dipping in and out of aspects of the island's history and interpreting certain events in a way calculated to amuse as well as inform.

Through the camera lens, this book also leaves no doubt that the Isle of Man is blessed with a truly wonderful natural environment. And if anywhere in the western world provides individuals, families and businesses with the ideal opportunities and freedom in which to flourish, the Isle of Man is it.

This is why I, like so many other Manx people I know, feel genuinely privileged to live and work here on the Isle of Man. And such is my passion for the place that I look forward to sending copies of *Three Legs in the Irish Sea* to friends and relatives who live 'across' – my way of showing off the very special island nation which my family and I are lucky enough to call home.

Happy reading!

Chris Hall,
Managing Director, Manx Telecom

Cashtal yn Ard dates from about 2000 BC – long before the concept of seaside holidays as we know them ever saw the light of day. It is a Neolithic long barrow (confusingly, nothing to do with gardening) – a series of burial chambers originally covered by a mound of earth and stone, rather than in this nude state.

No sea in sight – but it's not far away. Sulby Glen in spring epitomises the true beauty of the Isle of Man's landscape and its great attraction to visitors ever since the Victorians discovered the Irish Sea's 'new world'.

7

In 18th-century Britain, revolution was in the air. By the middle of

the 19th century, there was no stopping it. The wheels of industry

were taking people to places undreamed of as a new-found freedom

gave rise to the mantra:

ONE

We do like to be beside the seaside

So when did it all begin, this British love for the seaside and the subsequent 'discovery' of the Isle of Man?

It depends on how far back you want to go. But in broad brush-stroke terms, the Isle of Man obviously came first – in its present form, as an island separated from the land mass of Britain, about 12,000 years ago, give or take 500.

The earliest evidence of human habitation on the infant island points to 3,000 years after this, and judging by the large number of flint tools which these people left behind they certainly didn't spend their days lazing in the sun. On the other hand, being sprawled out on the beach must have been a distinct possibility, albeit as the gruesome leftovers of some hungry predator's lunch, but dismiss this thought immediately as it doesn't really sit too comfortably with the concept of the great British seaside holiday.

To understand the origins of buckets, spades and sand castles, you need look no further back than the middle of the 18th century. The idea grew from a treatise published by a Doctor Russell, extolling the virtues and life-affirming qualities of sea water – not merely bathing in it but heating it, or mixing it with milk, and drinking it.

Drink sea water? Surely the good doctor had been drinking something else, and too much of it, to suggest any such thing, particularly bearing

IT MUST HAVE BEEN THAT DIRTY OLD BUOY ON THE BEACH!

The first point to make about this postcard is that the outraged male is not necessarily referring to the man in the hat who has his back to them. The second point is that this kind of seaside humour was frowned upon by the Manx establishment to the point of censorship. From 1913, sauce was allowed on breakfast plates but definitely not on postcards for fear of moral corruption. Only cards approved by committee went on sale. Visiting holidaymakers were far more liberal, as revealed by the fetching beachwear (including that hat) shown (left) on Douglas sands.

SAILINGS AND HOLIDAY TOURS
1925

The Isle of Man Steam Packet Co Ltd
(Incorporated in the Isle of Man)

in mind the unspeakable (and indeed silent) added ingredient which ever-generous bathers have always been so relieved to donate.

Barmier still, he had the bottle to claim – and presumably believe – that sea water's medicinal powers were sufficient to cure ills such as deafness, consumption, rheumatism, asmtha and cancer. It's all too easy to scoff now, in the light of our vastly superior knowledge, but even in those days he couldn't have sounded like the sort of medical expert you'd readily trust as the ship's doctor. Not unless you were happy for your next destination to be the Dead Sea.

And yet, in response to Dr Russell's assertion that bathing in sea water was beneficial to health,

no less a luminary than the King of England declared it a splendid idea. Whereupon royalty took to it like ducks. In the process they splashed the south coast both into the news and on to the map, transforming Weymouth, Brighton and Eastbourne into highly fashionable resorts. For the rich, posh and pretentious compelled to follow in the monarch's footsteps, the seaside was most definitely the new place to be seen.

All very fine for the dandy – but what about mere ordinary mortals? When did the magic of the seaside happen for the great unwashed? To find out you have to wind the clock on another hundred years or so – to a time of great social and industrial revolution. Railways rather than

Above: Knickers to censorship!

Left: Far more respectable: the famous sunken gardens on Douglas promenade.

11

More chips with your Manx shearwater, madam?

One thing you *won't* find on the menu these days, either in the Port Erin cafe or any other eating establishment on the island, is Manx shearwater – a seabird so called because the species was first identified (in the 16th century) on the Isle of Man.

Yet at one time these small ground-nesting birds, which spend most of their life at sea, were regarded as a delicacy, taken from their burrows on the Calf of Man and salted, pickled and served. There was other commercial value in them too. Their oil was used to treat wool, and the softness and warmth of their feathers made perfect stuffing for bedding and cushions. And when the Manx shearwater population on the Calf was decimated by rats, clown-faced puffins (everyone's favourite seabird) involuntarily stepped in to keep the business ticking over – although you could hardly add 'nicely'.

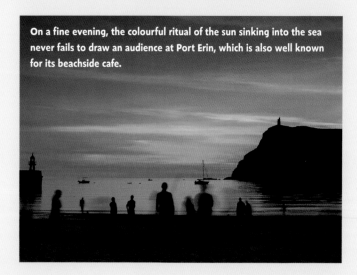

On a fine evening, the colourful ritual of the sun sinking into the sea never fails to draw an audience at Port Erin, which is also well known for its beachside cafe.

royalty started things moving, opening the way for coastal towns in the north to rise above their station by daring to dream, prosper and flourish.

'The coming of the railways' is an expression often used to paint the picture at a stroke of a Britain magically transformed by a rattling good transport system. Of course, it didn't happen overnight, but it certainly made an exciting new world of fast local and regional travel accessible and affordable to many, and enabled the working classes of Lancashire's booming industrial towns to make tracks to well-publicised Blackpool and its many inviting attractions.

The relevance of Blackpool is that as well as being on England's Irish Sea coast, it quickly became synonymous with a heady combination of bracing sea air and all the fun of the fair. Entertainment in one form or another was on and around every street corner, and in time the beaches, piers, theatres, Golden Mile and the north-west's answer to the Eiffel Tower were destined to make the words seaside holiday and Blackpool one and the same thing for a sizeable chunk of Britain's population. Yet in the early days of this tourism boom, cheap and cheerful were never on the agenda in some quarters of Blackpool. Aspirations were keenly focused on emulating the success of those posh southern places such as Brighton and Eastbourne by pandering to the needs of the gentry and middle classes.

At the same time, the fruit-machine eyeballs of successful money-making industrialists and

Left top: The stokers are working their socks off aboard *Princess Victoria*, a ship built for Manx Line in 1887 and which entered Steam Packet service in 1888.

Left botton: The first Isle of Man Steam Packet ship to bear the name *Lady of Mann* made her maiden voyage in 1930 and bowed out gracefully in 1971.

entrepreneurs were dizzily clicking up the pound signs in true Disney cartoon fashion as they witnessed a voracious appetite for seaside holidays, fun and entertainment – the perfect antidote to the pressures of the daily grind of the north-west's mills and factories.

And with the Irish Sea coast growing in popularity, not too far away was another potential gem waiting to be polished – the Isle of Man.

Even without the polishing, the Isle of Man carried the promise of a holiday destination with extra sparkle – the lure of a world all on its own, separate, self-contained, accessible only by sea, and about which, off island, very little was known. Travelling there and back would be an adventure in itself – an opportunity for ordinary Joe Soap to feel the same thrill of setting foot on a land unexplored in the style of Mungo Park,

Far left: In the 1860s, residents of Castletown were not exactly over the moon with the idea that the island's ancient capital should lose its status to that young upstart town Douglas, which has remained the capital ever since.

Left top: Over the centuries, the peninsula at Langness had wickedly drawn many ships to a watery grave before the lighthouse came along in 1880 to brighten things up.

Left bottom: The industrious Victorians invented many interesting things, one of the most popular – certainly as a seaside attraction – being the clever camera obscura, of which very few now remain. Hence this restored and reopened example on Douglas Head is all the more intriguing.

Far left: On a fine summer day, Peel appeal makes it as popular with trippers as it is for its famous traditional Manx kippers. In the background are the old fishing port's medieval castle and cathedral ruins, the story of which is told in the House of Manannan – an interactive heritage centre which although a world apart from these historic monuments is located on the waterfront just a short distance away.

Left: From Peel, a little further south on the west coast is Port Erin, a resort boasting the very ingredients that first made British seaside holidays such a hit – golden sands, safe seas, a sheltered bay and glorious sunsets. It is also the southern terminus of the Isle of Man Steam Railway, where an interesting museum greets you at the station.

Far left: Luxuries which were beyond the means and imagination of those early tourists – pleasure boats pontooned in the new marina at Douglas.

Left: Myth, folklore and superstition are rife on the Isle of Man, and at a certain time in a certain light, alone on a deserted beach, it is all too easy to ponder the presence of prying eyes and the muted cry of voices long departed whispering on the wind. And is that the shimmering outline of a pale longship ghosting silently towards you?

Henry Morton Stanley and other great British explorers of the era – but without the fear of being sacrificed in a boiling stew pot and served up by the natives.

On the subject of hot water, in 1830 the Isle of Man Steam Packet Company was formed, connecting Douglas and Liverpool by, initially, regular though infrequent sailings. The first single fares cost the princely sum of three shillings (fifteen pence!) or five shillings (twenty-five pence) if you wanted to travel in the toffs' seats. Almost 180 years on, the Steam Packet is the oldest passenger ship company in the world still trading under its original name.

So with trains to get you to the ships and ships to get you to Douglas, the Isle of Man also became part of the great British seaside holiday phenomenon. And, naturally, important developments were soon afoot on the island – many of them along Douglas seafront and adjoining streets and terraces – to accommodate and entertain this welcome invasion of visitors.

Douglas harbour acquired the new Victoria Pier in 1873 so that ferries could come alongside instead of anchoring in the bay. In the same year, the Isle of Man Steam Railway opened its first

19

Looking at this stunning view over Port Erin and the wild west coast, you wouldn't argue with the claim that as much as 40% of the island's land area is uninhabited.

Look out! She's watching us – and she's not amused.

All the records say that Blackpool Tower was built as England's answer to the Eiffel Tower. But is this just another conspiracy theory? Is the real truth (as suggested by some) that Blackpool Tower was erected on the express orders of Queen Victoria to keep an eye on the Isle of Man? It all makes sense.

Queen Victoria (they say) grew up hating the sea, the seaside, seafarers (including, irrationally, Vikings) and most of all Doctor Russell. In her eyes the bad doctor had killed her father, who died when she was just eight months old after he had taken a stroll on Sidmouth beach. His intention was to catch a breath of sea air (the health benefits of which had been widely extolled by the doctor) but instead he caught a fatal dose of pneumonia.

Then came the episode which made an already nervous Victoria (who not only inherited the job Queen of England but also Lord of Man) even more suspicious. Castletown was losing its status as

the island's capital, the role passing to Douglas. Why? She reasoned that from Douglas it would be a simple matter for those Manx nationals who resented English rule to launch a fleet of longships and invade the Lancashire coast. Hence her cunning plan to install that very tall lookout tower at Blackpool and cast a watchful eye across the Irish Sea for any sign of trouble.

Queen Victoria had indicated her unease at being Lord of Man some years earlier, when the Royal Yacht *Britannia* anchored in Ramsey Bay en route from a holiday cruise in Scotland. She was invited ashore but made some excuse about not having had her hair done and sent Prince Albert in her place. Imagine her surprise when he came back in one piece, praising the Manx for their warmth and hospitality.

Furthermore, her unashamed favouritism for the Isle of Wight was already well known. She spent many a long (and no doubt outrageous) weekend at the big white Cowes house of mad Ozzy Osbourne.

Photo courtesy of Visit Blackpool

Blackpool Tower is more than 500 feet (152 m) tall – much higher than needed if its intended purpose was anything other than to see over the distant horizon and keep a beady eye on Douglas harbour.

21

Above: It wouldn't be the Irish Sea without views of Ireland – such as this one of the lovely Mountains of Mourne.

Far right: Proving that the west coast doesn't have the monopoly on dramatic seascapes: east-coast Garwick Bay in the foreground, Laxey Head in the near distance and, between the two, the entrance to Laxey harbour.

line – coast to coast, east to west, Douglas to Peel. Other railways and tramways followed: the Manx Electric Railway, the Snaefell Mountain Railway, the Groudle Glen Railway, the Douglas Southern Electric Tramway and Douglas's cable and horse tramways.

A lot of railway for a little kingdom? Not when you consider that the majority of these systems became part of the island's public transport services, appreciated and lauded by visitors as well as locals. Reinvestment in maintenance and improvements has managed to keep most of the services running, and their Victorian and Edwardian appeal still endures today. It was not by coincidence that the golden age of British seaside holidays was also the golden age of Britain's railways.

In 1913 the number of summer visitors to the Isle of Man topped the 615,000 mark – a record. The outlook was bright, but the awful spectre of the First World War was casting an ever-blacker shadow over the Manx landscape.

On an island with an unfamiliar tongue, and much talk

of long-held superstitions and fears, it's all too easy to

say the wrong thing.

TWO

Mind your language

On the morning of 21st July 1969, people living on, in or alongside the Irish Sea must have been flabbergasted to a point way beyond gobsmacked when, sleepily tucking into their toast and newspapers, they found themselves greeted by the truly awesome headline *MAN CONQUERS THE MOON*.

Spontaneous reactions from around the Irish Sea varied somewhat – from the enormously proud "We did it! We did it! That's the old Viking spirit for you!" to the tax-paying more cynical "So *that's* what Tynwald's been spending our money on" to the cringingly jealous "Well it's hardly rocket science is it."

And then, apart from for those who'd already choked on their toast in the excitement, how Manx pride must have been just as quickly deflated when the real story behind that cruelly ambiguous headline revealed itself, Man referring not to the Isle of but to Man the human race – and to American specimens at that, aboard a ship called *Apollo 11* which was obviously a world beyond anything the Steam Packet could ever hope to muster.

It's a story which sharply illustrates the very annoying ability of language to mislead and confuse. How does it do this? And why? What is language anyway? Where did it come from?

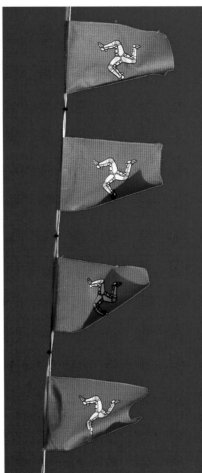

In the company of such an abundance of famous three legs, you couldn't be anywhere else but the Isle of Man – although it should be noted that Her Majesty Queen Elizabeth II, Lord of Man, has only two.

Right top: **Are the traditional three legs above the entrance at Ronaldsway Airport a reminder to get a move on to avoid missing your flight?**

Right bottom: **Isle of Man history displays many interesting milestones, as does the landscape.**

To answer this inevitably means digging into some dark corner or other of history, which unfortunately is littered with dead people, and plenty of them, the vast majority of whom were either too preoccupied with their own lives or just too lazy to write anything down. They had absolutely no thought for all the time and trouble we'd have to go to today, poking around for scraps about how they lived and what they did and who with and why and where and how often.

Various excuses have been made on their behalf for this annoying state of affairs.

They were too busy fighting off other tribes who wanted their land, cattle and women.

They were otherwise engaged hunting for food, scratching a living and building homesteads.

They were just so focused on protecting their families and children, and keeping famine, starvation, disease, weather and predators at bay, that the simple and relaxing task of writing a diary every day was apparently beyond them. Ridiculous! Had these people never heard of multi-tasking?

The wise and elders of the village didn't help either, foolishly claiming that when the time came for future generations to be obsessed with tracing their family trees and such like – not to mention finding out something useful about language – they would only have to type in 'Google' and it would be job done.

Hence the situation today, and the confusion that confronts you when you start thinking just a little more deeply about that rush of early holidaymakers crossing the Irish Sea with the

Steam Packet, clutching their buckets and spades. How excited they must have been at the prospect of stepping ashore a virtually foreign land, armed with little more knowledge than it was called the Isle of Man, and looking forward to meeting him.

And then it hits you: what language would greet their arrival at Douglas? English? Manx Gaelic? Norse? Would any conversation be possible, or would grunts, expressions and spontaneous sign language have to suffice? Thanks to our selfish and thoughtless non-writing forebears, the picture is not exactly clear.

This is because one version of history quite clearly states that up until the 19th century (1800 in round numbers) English was a foreign language to most Manx people. Against this, the 1901 census revealed the population to be more than 54,600, of whom only 8% (4,400 plus) claimed any knowledge of their native tongue, let alone the ability to speak it (fluently or otherwise). So is a mere hundred years really enough to virtually wipe out a language hitherto spoken for centuries?

And then there are other somewhat contradictory facts suggested by history, such as the island's upper classes all speaking good English as early as the mid 17th century (1650ish for argument's sake) while the lower classes (those who lived out in the sticks tending the land and livestock and manning the fishing boats, i.e. doing all the dirty jobs and in all weathers to keep the grub on the table) spoke Manx Gaelic. This state of affairs no doubt gave the latter unlimited opportunities to curse their masters to

Left bottom: Somewhere in Manx folklore it probably explains the significance of a Loaghtan sheep giving you the V-sign (albeit with its horns) while you photograph it.

Or maybe it's a display of smug superiority, Loaghtan lamb being a product awarded the prestigious European PDO (Designation of Origin) stamp, signifying that it is as unique as Champagne, Parma Ham and Camembert.

The breed has evolved on the Isle of Man over thousands of years and the meat has a highly individual flavour and is low in fat and cholesterol. And, unlike Manx shearwater and puffin, Loaghtan lamb is available on menus across the island.

Far right: A grand example of the three legs symbol in all its finery, complete with spurs. But then, this is the site of the Great Laxey Wheel – a giant memorial to the Isle of Man's rich mining heritage.

Striking!

This photograph shows the home of Tynwald, the Manx parliament, in the heart of Douglas.

Known locally as the Wedding Cake, it's a building you can hardly miss – but it's not as striking as the lightning which in the 1950s hit the flagpole on historic Tynwald Hill in St John's and split it in two!

Fortunately, it didn't happen on Tynwald Day. It was just one of those flash-in-the-pan examples of extreme weather which occasionally lash out in the Irish Sea.

their faces without fear of retribution, making for hilarious drinking sessions in the pub when recalling such moments for the entertainment of their Manx-speaking mates, but it doesn't really help us in our quest. Confuses is more the word that screams to mind.

And then you can throw something else into the pot: the suggestion that the strong English influence, albeit for the privileged, was not altogether surprising given that Queen Elizabeth I, whose dad was of course Henry VIII, became Lord of Man many years before this – in 1594. But hang on a mo' – didn't that lot all speak Latin in those days?

If you haven't blown a head gasket by now, you never will. So maybe it's time to give up gracefully and tell your enquiring mind that it's in a queue and will be dealt with as soon as a brain cell becomes available – but not before noting that also apparently supporting the idea that English was fairly well established in relation to Manx was the fact that very little of Manx Gaelic was ever committed to print, exceptions being a Bible and prayer book (both 18th century) and a Manx dictionary (19th century).

As for all the incredible and enduring tales of Manx myth, legend and folklore, these were passed on verbally from one generation to the next, in the great tradition of storytellers since time and stories began. Or so they say.

There's also no doubt that English came to dominate because it was the language of trade and administration, piling further social, economic and political pressure on the survival of

Manx Gaelic. But there was a will and determination that survive it must, and the formation in 1899 of the Manx Language Society (Yn Cheshaght Ghailckagh) was an important step.

More than a century later, in a shrinking world of blurred boundaries, it is not only minority languages which are under threat but the very fabric of national identities, traditions and cultures. So all those people on the Isle of Man who are pouring their energies into initiatives in education, art, literature, crafts, music and events must be mightily relieved that the future for the Manx Gaelic language looks secure. And that's not just talk.

Far left: The heather-clad area of Eary Cushlin on the west coast is National Trust property and combines stunning views with the site of the island's most isolated keeill – Lag ny Keeilley (the hollow of the chapel).

Left top: The Tower of Refuge in Douglas Bay provided a haven for shipwrecked sailors caught out on the treacherous approach to the harbour. The tower was the initiative of Sir William Hillary, who also laid the foundations for the creation of the Royal National Lifeboat Institution.

Left bottom: Never mind shipwrecked – in the dead of winter you wouldn't want to be landwrecked, not in these remote hills. Such an ordeal would undoubtedly inspire some pretty colourful language – Manx Gaelic, English or any other!

Wash your mouth out!

- **The F word** is one of two which are guaranteed to cause enormous offence – not to mention the prospect of dire consequences.

  The Isle of Man's fairy folklore is as old as Manannan himself, but the Little People get very annoyed when referred to as fairies, much preferring Themselves. Upsetting them could mean being taken and never seen again. On the bright side, saying or waving a cheery greeting to them as you cross the Fairy Bridge (itself very inappropriately named, given the tradition) will put you in their good books and no harm should come to you.

- **The R word** is just as likely to guarantee you appalling bad luck – in fact, infest you with it. So powerful is the Manx superstition that it's even forbidden to use the word in print. Suffice to say that the creature in question is a rodent, has four legs (not three), and is bigger than a mouse. Can you tell what it is yet? If so, don't say it out loud – not if you're on the Isle of Man at the time!

  So spare a thought for those members of the Manx Regiment who, in 1942, must have been quaking in their boots on discovering that they were being posted overseas – to fight with the Desert Rats!

- **Disgraceful, Miss!** Has our everyday language changed much since the 1930s? Apparently. As two young sweethearts from Scotland sat enjoying each other's company near Douglas, a local man shot the boyfriend and tried to throw the girl over the cliffs as she screamed at him, "You are a darned rotter!" Steady on, old girl! After all, a chap was only trying to murder you.

Traditional ways of life and Manx crafts and culture are remembered and kept alive at Cregneash – a village of whitewashed thatched cottages preserved as a permanent reminder of how things were for a 19th-century crofting community.

Cregneash was also the home of Manx-speaking Harry Kelly. After he died (1930s), a member of his family donated his cottage to the nation as a museum, and it continues to fascinate visitors almost 80 years on and will probably do so for many more to come.

By 1961 only 165 of the island's population claimed to speak Manx Gaelic. The last native speaker was Ned Maddrell, but by the time of his death in 1974 there was already great interest in reviving the language. Efforts to do so have grown to the extent that it is now an option in the island's primary schools.

Far left: Gathering in the corn – without the aid of modern farming methods and machinery. That beaming smile probably wasn't the standard expression while performing such a back-breaking task.

Left: A case of too much ale at the Cregneash Arms? No – a bit of traditional singing and dancing for the entertainment of summer visitors.

35.

This Viking didn't miss the last longship home – he's on permanent
display in Peel's House of Manannan.

Meanwhile, a Cregneash resident helps to maintain the village's much-treasured calm and tranquillity by smoking a peace pipe.

GUARD

Bliss! Trains and trams and boats and planes

– and so many ways to go.

Across the sea and over the hills

Throughout the past century, more than a few observers have suggested – not unkindly – that the Isle of Man would be more appropriately named the Isle of Mad.

Mad, that is, about transport.

For such a small place – approximately 33 miles (53 km) long by 13.5 miles (22 km) at its widest point – Man is something of a transport enthusiasts' paradise and, equally, a tranquillity seekers' paradox: a unique living heritage museum on one hand and a world-beating motorsports centre on the other, all rolled out across one very green, very pleasant and very relaxing rock in the Irish Sea, where pace of life varies between the extremes of as lazy as a Loaghtan sheep to as manic as a 200-miles-an-hour TT bike.

To any island community, transport is the physical link with the 'outside' world, the only means of getting from one to the other. And until 'Beam me up, Scottie' becomes a reality, or somebody with the vast financial resources of a Premiership footballer builds two Channel-style Irish Sea tunnels (or 60-mile Isle of Skye-style bridges), the only way to get to and from the Isle of Man from the east coast of Ireland or west coast of England, or beyond of course, will be by air or sea.

Hardly surprising then that boats, ships, aircraft and even balloons have played such a

If you want to see the deepest and one of the most dramatic of the Isle of Man's 17 national glens, the Manx Electric Railway will deliver you to the entrance. Dhoon Glen is 2 miles (3 km) north of Laxey, and the walk from the station (600 feet/183 metres above sea level) down to the bay is a very satisfying way to spend 30 minutes or so. En route through the ravine you will see the spectacular two-drop waterfall.

The railway also takes you conveniently close to beautiful Ballaglass Glen, which is a little further north and not far from Maughold Head. According to Manx folklore, this is the haunt of the Londhoo – a giant Irish deer. It's not an entirely fanciful idea, as the Royal Scottish Museum in Edinburgh displays the skeleton of a great deer, sometimes referred to as an Irish elk, dug up by a Manx farmer at Ballaugh in 1819. And another and much better example was later discovered at St John's. It can be seen in the Manx Museum in Douglas.

significant role in the very colourful story of Manx transport, some of the most incredible chapters of which were written in the years of both wars.

For example, who would believe that a humble ferry, albeit one temporarily converted to a troop carrier, could sink a lethal warship? Obviously not the captain of the German U-boat which surfaced almost dead ahead of the Steam Packet's seconded paddle steamer *Mona's Queen* in the English Channel in 1917 and fired a torpedo at her.

The torpedo missed but *Mona's Queen* retaliated in true Viking spirit by maintaining course and ramming the U-boat's conning tower, causing severe damage and forcing the disabled sub to dive immediately and stay out of further harm's way. *Mona's Queen* captain and crew were later awarded a princely (in those days) sum of £300 for their actions.

Other Steam Packet ships and crews doing their duty for king and country weren't so lucky. In the Second World War, three vessels were lost at Dunkirk alone. Of the many other crew members who survived their war experiences, some at least had the consolation of being awarded medals for outstanding bravery.

The history of Manx air travel is obviously much briefer. The first Man'd (so to speak) flight was a momentous occasion in November 1902 when 45,000 cubic feet of gas wrapped in a balloon 60 feet high carried two men from Douglas almost 80 miles to Dumfrieshire in Scotland – an epic four-and-a-half-hour aerial

adventure. The two basket cases (as they must have seemed) were Percival Spencer and Reverend Bacona.

It was another seventeen years before Isle of Man aviation history was made again – and this time in an aeroplane piloted by Manx war hero Captain Elgie Jefferson of the RAF. In January 1919 he became the first Manxman to fly across the Irish Sea to the Isle of Man, taking off from Hooton near Ellesmere Port and touching down on the island 40 minutes later close to Ballasalla. Unfortunately the story doesn't have a happy ending. In the same year a crash in the English Channel ended the 23-year-old's short but groundbreaking life.

In 1919, other significant pioneering achievements were in the air. One was in the shape of the R34, the world's largest airship, passing over the Isle of Man on a round-Ireland trip.

Another was the arrival of a new craze called pleasure flying. For the considerable cost of one guinea (one pound and a shilling, or one pound five pence today), you and another passenger could see Douglas Bay as you'd never seen it before, from on high. And one of those to take advantage of such an unmissable opportunity was singer Florrie Ford, who for many years enjoyed enormous popularity with summer audiences on the island.

Then there was the first commercial flight to Man – early-morning delivery of the *Daily News*, flown in to Douglas from Lake Windermere. The pilot was a bit of a newsmaker himself: Captain Howard Pixton, who five years earlier, in 1914,

Left: Derby Castle at the north end of Douglas promenade is the terminus of the Manx Electric Railway, the other terminus being 17 miles away at Ramsey. If this picture dates from 1931 or later, it couldn't have been taken on a Sunday – photography on the Sabbath was declared illegal in 1931, and many other harmless pleasures were already prohibited. Perhaps holidaymakers stayed out of trouble by going to bed on Saturday night and not getting up until Monday morning.

Middle: A Thomas the Tank impersonator?
Not quite. More a popular Santa Special on the Isle of Man Steam Railway – the kind of regular festive event which helps to encourage out-of-season visitors.

Left below: "Hey! Come back with our favourite pantomime horse! We'd recognise Reg Rash anywhere!" But is the fine specimen cutting a dash along Douglas prom who they really think it is? And will chapter six reveal all?

41

The narrow-gauge Isle of Man Steam Railway is perfectly scaled to recreate the magic of Reverend Awdry's famous character – and where better to host special Thomas the Tank Weekends than in the very place which inspired his fictional home?

Thomas the Tank of Sodor

- The creator of Thomas the Tank Engine and friends was the Reverend W. Awdry – author, clergyman and railway enthusiast.

- Born in Romsey, Hampshire, in 1911, the son of a clergyman, he was awarded the OBE in 1996 and died peacefully in Stroud, Gloucestershire, in 1997.

- A British Rail Class 91 diesel locomotive, 91 124, is named in his honour.

- The first book, *The Three Railway Engines*, was published in 1945. By 1972 there were 26 books in *The Railway Series* and son Christopher subsequently added more.

- The setting for the stories is Sodor – a fictional island in the Irish Sea, inspired by a visit to the Isle of Man.

- Reverend Awdry and his brother George worked out the history, geography, industry and language of Sodor between them, in incredible detail, their abridged notes published in a book entitled *The Island of Sodor: Its People, History and Railways* (Kaye and Ward 1986).

- The place names on Sodor are mostly a mixture of Manx and Norse and the island's language is Sudric.

- A 2008 survey by the National Autistic Society concluded that the adventures of Thomas and his friends are educationally valuable to autistic children, helping them to distinguish emotions, colours, numbers and words.

Left top: Mining at Laxey began in about 1780 and continued through to the 1920s. Shafts were more than 2,000 feet (610 metres) deep and the zinc ore was carried from the mines by a tramway and taken to the washing floors to be prepared for sale. From 1877 this work was done by two small narrow-gauge steam locomotives called *Ant* and *Bee*. Part of the surface section of the tramway has been restored and two replica locomotives transport passengers on the journey once taken by the mined minerals, terminating within easy walking distance of the Great Laxey Wheel.

Left bottom: A horse tram advertising car hire looks a little bit like shooting yourself in the foot, but the horse isn't complaining. It keeps him (or her) in a job and it's better than walking the streets. The horse trams (but not the horse) date back to 1876. These days it's a summer-only service.

Questions…

1 Complete the following list: Fenella, Sutherland, Derby, Pender, Peveril, Loch, Mona and Tynwald.

2 What was the connection between them?

3 Which attraction now occupies land that was once part of the station at Peel?

4 There was a six-year period in which the Isle of Man Steam Railway consistently carried more than a million passengers per annum. When was this?

5 Horse tram cars which had an iron arch at each end, but no roof, were called what?

6 Have diesels ever run on the Isle of Man Steam Railway?

7 The Second World War saw the temporary suspension of Douglas horse tram services. In which year did they resume?

...and answers.

1 Thornhill, Caledonia, Douglas, Maitland, G.H. Wood, Hutchinson, Kissack and Mannin.

2 They were all steam locomotives of the Isle of Man Railway.

3 The House of Manannan interactive heritage centre.

4 During the years of the Second World War (1939 to 1945).

5 Toast racks.

6 Yes. In 1961 two diesel railcars dating from 1950 were purchased from County Donegal Railways. It was thought that their low running costs would make off-season services a viable proposition.

7 1946.

Main photo: Signs – as well as newspaper headlines! – can be so ambiguous. Does the word on the carriage door identify this man as the guard? Or is it an instruction to guard him for all you're worth? It must be the former. He looks far too friendly to be dangerous.

45

There can't be many places in the British Isles where two popular seaside resorts sit back to back along one short stretch of the same beautiful, looping coastline. This is the happy position of Port Erin (foreground) and Port St Mary in the south-west corner of the Isle of Man. And beyond lies the wild beauty of the Langness peninsula, where many bird species, including chough (increasingly rare elsewhere in Britain), are in their element.

Top: Departing soon: the Isle of Man Steam Railway's next Douglas to Port Erin train, calling at Castletown (and any other station or halt as passengers and the timetable dictate).
The gleaming locomotive, a masterclass in pride, spit and polish, is named *Loch* (as in Sir Henry).

had won the Schneider Trophy for England.

So much for the first leg of the exciting Isle of Man adventure – getting to the island.

What about the most intriguing prospect of all – exploring this newly-discovered mystical (and often mistical) foreign yet in many ways familiarly British land of myth and legend? In the early days of tourism, how would you go about it? With the notable exception of the motor car, the short answer is much as you would today.

Take trains, for instance. When it comes to railways, the Isle of Mad is crazy about them – and has been since 1873 with the opening of a line between Douglas and Peel. This no longer exists, but the additional Douglas to Castletown and Port Erin route which opened a year later is not only still running but has received massive 21st-century reinvestment in new track, signalling and improved safety measures.

Other Victorian survivors going strong today are the Manx Electric Railway (1893) and Snaefell Mountain Railway (1895).

And not to be left behind are the horses coming up on the rails – the Douglas promenade trams (1876). Such was their popularity that by the end of the first decade of the 20th century there were 45 horse trams in service, annual passenger numbers rising towards the near two million mark. That's an awful lot of buckets to fill – and goes some way to explaining why Douglas's fine seafront gardens have always come up roses.

Compared with the railways, the island's roads in the late 19th century must have been much quieter, motor cars – such as they were – being a

rich man's toy and traffic jams occurring only when two horses and carts were competing to get through the same gateway. And what a boon the bicycle must have been for the common man!

So if the railways were providing public transport, what about buses? Well they arrived late, not offering a challenge to the train monopoly until 1927. In between times it was the age and coming of the charabanc – in the 1920s an extended roofless motor car, the most capacious offering as many as 28 passengers the eye-opening experience of an Isle of Man summer excursion. Fitted with new-fangled pneumatic tyres, 'charas' were a thrilling advance in road travel compared with traditional horsedrawn carriages and wagonettes, despite the 12 mph speed limit. 'Do' the island in a day became such a popular proposition that the Steam Packet cashed in with five 'round the island' sailings a week.

Other interesting milestones in the development of Manx road transport included the installation in 1932 of the island's first traffic lights (at an accident blackspot in Douglas) and the arrival, in 1946, of the first double decker bus.

And from 1907 onwards, gathering momentum all the time and in every sense was the crowd-pulling spectacle for which the Isle of Man was to achieve astonishing and enduring worldwide fame – the TT. If anything could support the idea of the island being justly referred to as the Isle of Mad, this was definitely it.

Bottom: Arriving: the Steam Packet's *Lady of Mann*, steering well clear of the Conister Rock reef, marked so clearly by the Tower of Refuge, on the approach into Douglas harbour.

Can the southern uplands of Scotland really be this close to the Isle of Man? Surprisingly (to many first-time visitors), yes. Unfortunately there isn't a ferry service connecting the two, but this view of Ramsey Bay and the Point of Ayre emphasises that Man is much nearer to Scotland than it is to England. To the far right of the picture is the Albert Tower which stands above Ramsey – a memorial to the unannounced visit in 1847 of Queen Victoria (who hid under the bed covers and stayed onboard *Britannia*) and Prince Albert (who went ashore).

An extremely odd number of bizarre,

extraordinary and fascinating things.

Three recurring

What has three legs, twelve feet but never moves?

The answer stands outside the entrance to Ronaldsway Airport. It is Manxman Bryan Kneale's bronze sculpture, created as part of the 1979 Tynwald Millennium celebrations, and it depicts the famous triskelion – the Isle of Man's very distinctive three legs symbol.

To say that it never moves is not strictly true. When it was unveiled as a thought-provoking work of art, twelve feet high, the sculpture moved those who questioned its very unorthodox view of the three legs. In simultaneously embracing the concept of flight the legs are skeletal and propellor-like in profile, and of course three-dimensional – visually, far removed from the strength and union implicit in the traditional armoured and spurred legs so often depicted on a solid flat surface.

The controversy serves as a reminder that even in a century of great change, particularly in the population mix, the Manx are a very proud people. You only have to see the proliferation of three legs symbols all over the island to know that. They are everywhere – on doors, gates, walls and windows of just about every sort of building – and in a great variety of forms and designs.

In fact, even a whole building took its design inspiration from the three legs. The Sea

Manx cats have found fans and favour around the world, including the rich and famous – and including Walt Disney! And all this despite being a notoriously difficult breed.

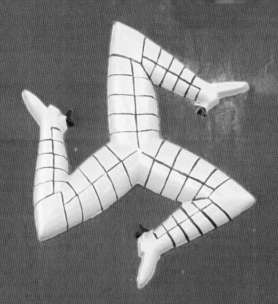

If this particular example of the triskelion happens to be a door bell, it'll take a very tall postman to ring it.

Small, but very apeeling!

Still officially recognised by no less an authority than the *Guinness Book of World Records* as the smallest road-legal car ever produced, the Peel P50 was launched at the 1962 Earls Court Motorcycle Show in London. In 1963 it cost £199 – a whopping (at the time) £50 cheaper than the going price of a good motorbike.

It was in fact classed as a motorcycle, with three wheels, no speedo, a single-cylinder 49 cc engine and automatic three-speed forward gearbox. To reverse it you had to get out and physically turn it round using a chrome handle on the rear – a very easy matter because the lightweight fibreglass body was well under half a ton. This aspect was highlighted on *Top Gear* in traffic-jammed London streets as other drivers looked on with envy and no little amazement. The maximum speed of 40 mph, combined with 100-miles-a-gallon economy, further demonstrated that the P50 would make the perfect city

car today – hence the clamour of interest from prospective owners desperate to get their hands on one.

Unless it goes back into production, they are destined for disappointment. Just 100 P50s were made. Every one was hand built, with individual variations that made it not only unique but, more than 40 years on, highly collectable and valuable.

On the Isle of Man there are only two P50s, one of which is privately owned and the other – a 1962 model – on display in Peel Transport Museum. It was bought in Cheshire in 2004. The total cost of bringing it home was £10,500, and it has since been lovingly restored.

The P50 – the only car ever manufactured on the Isle of Man – was the brainchild and creation of Cyril Cannell and Henry Kissack. At the height of production their Peel Engineering Company employed 40 people.

Export sales included America where, on its test run to satisfy the Bureau of Transportation, the inspector rolled the P50 down an embankment. Disaster? No! Escaping without a scratch, he passed it immediately as suitable for use !

Terminal, which since 1965 has welcomed passengers arriving at Douglas harbour, is in the shape of three curved arms.

The triskelion has been around for a long time, in use in Sicily as early as the end of the 7th century BC (and still used there today) and very likely associated with the Isle of Man since at least the 10th century AD, although the earliest known representation of it on the island dates from the 14th century. Yet it was not until 1932 that the symbol was sanctioned for use on the island's national flag. The three legs also feature as the centrepiece for a new coat of arms granted to the Isle of Man by Royal Warrant in 1996.

Of course, no one really believes that a Manxman (or a Sicilian) has three legs, any more than a Scotsman has a secret weapon under his kilt, or a Welshman has to stop at every town for a leek, or an Englishman goes out in the midday sun with a mad dog. But if it was true, and the three-legged race was an Olympic event, just imagine the Manx walking off with all those gold medals...

Far less fanciful is the idea that three is something of a recurring number on the Isle of Man. Take as an example the amazing three-wheeled Peel P50, the world's smallest car, which although built in the 1960s shot to renewed global fame in 2007 as BBC's *Top Gear* put it in the television spotlight and created enormous interest. Emails flooded in to the programme, many declaring, "I must have a P50, it's fantastic, where can I buy one?"

It further prompted the question that if three

wheels look like making a big revival, isn't it high time there was a Reliant Robin TT? Del Boy and Rodney would definitely be up for it, on account of their appetite for fast bucks.

Three was also an interesting figure in what was surely one of the most amazing sporting achievements of all time – a 1934 football match in which the Isle of Man chalked up a 7-3 away victory over Liverpool!

And then there was the equally astonishing rescue of a badly injured airman by Peg-leg – a farm dog with four legs but only three feet. It was the dog's persistent growling which led his owners to discover that a plane had crashed on a remote hillside in thick fog, leaving only one survivor from the six crew. The injured man had spent two days and nights in the open but thanks to the dog lived to tell the tale.

The subject of animals raises another question: when Curraghs Wildlife Park opened in 1965, did the animals go in three by three?

Other examples of the coincidence of three include the number of words in Isle of Man and the number of letters in Man. The latter also applies to cat (the tail-less variety of which is one of the island's biggest claims to fame) and its lesser-loved (in fact positively detested) infamous and unmentionable rhyming rodent.

No connection intended with the above, but Tynwald, the Manx parliament, is the only one in the world with three chambers.

The island has three coastlines: east, west and south, the north of the island effectively being only a point (Point of Ayre).

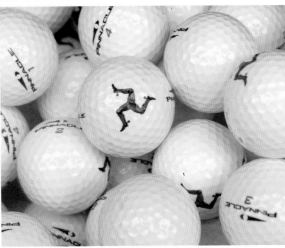

On the Isle of Man you just can't get away from those legs. They're everywhere: Isle of Man Bank (AD 1865), the Tynwald building and even as a secret weapon to help give Manx golfers the run of the green. And although that looks like a beach where the Manx flag is flying, it's actually the surface of the Moon! It's a little-known fact that Colonel Jim Irwin, *Apollo 15* astronaut and the first man to drive a moon buggy on the lunar surface (in 1971), was actually at the wheel of a Peel P50 on that momentous occasion – the purpose for which the world's smallest car was originally (but secretly) designed! This astonishing truth (some claim) came out when Colonel Irwin was guest of honour at the Isle of Man's 1979 Millennium Air Rally at Jurby Airfield. It all makes sense. And maybe it was this alleged revelation which helped inflate the price of a Peel P50 sold at auction in the UK in 1997 for a whopping £28,750!

The centre picture could be a particularly heavy session of kipper smoking at Peel, or Manannan's legendary cloak of mist drawing a veil over the island to frustrate prying eyes.

57

Right: Tynwald Day 2008. The Manx Sword of State, dating from the 12th or 13th century and since 1998 in the safe hands of the Royal British Legion's Bernadette McCabe (the first woman in history to be given the role of official swordbearer), emerges from the Royal Chapel at St John's on to the Processional Way. Presiding over the Tynwald Hill ceremony was Her Royal Highness the Princess Royal. It's all part of the pomp and ceremony which make the Isle of Man's national day celebrations such a special day in the calendar of annual events.

There are three major Victorian railways: Isle of Man Steam, Manx Electric and Snaefell Mountain.

Laxey displays three restored 'working' attractions which were key elements in the success of the island's once-rich mining industry: the Laxey Mines Railway, the Great Laxey Wheel (*Lady Isabella*) and the Snaefell Mine Waterwheel (*Lady Evelyn*).

The long sweeping crescent seafront at Douglas comprises three promenades: Loch, Harris and Central.

The island has three major entertainment venues: the restored Gaiety Theatre, the Villa Marina and Erin Arts Centre. On the same subject, the three Gibb brothers – Maurice, Robin and Barry, better known as the Bee Gees – were born in Douglas.

Mention of world-famous stars also brings the word tripod to mind – specifically, the kind used by photographers and by the movie cameras of the Isle of Man's not insignificant film and television production industry. And what's the strength of a tripod in providing perfect support for all kinds of optical equipment? The stability inherent in its shape.

So is this stability a simple explanation of how the Isle of Man, standing solid as a rock on its three legs, has managed to achieve more than a thousand years of continuous parliament?

It's easy to believe that this high and desolate place is known as **Windy Corner** – but perhaps a little more surprising to learn that it's a well-known (if not infamous) feature of the TT course, the gusts presenting yet another challenge to riders. This view is looking due south to Douglas and the east coast.

The three legs survive but it's a sad tail of an airline that is no more – Euromanx.

Top: Isle of Man bank notes were first issued in 1961, in denominations of ten shillings, £1 and £5. Those people keen to get their hands on a tenner or two had to wait awhile longer.

Above: Tynwald Day always attracts an intrigued audience.

Say it with flowers. Three legs stretched out in the gardens of Ramsey's Mooragh Park.

Its real name is Ballalona Bridge and it crosses the ford near Santon. Tradition has it that the area is haunted by the fairies who held the ford after battle, which is why it is regarded wise for any Manx person using the bridge to pay his or her respects. In recent years a new tradition has emerged. Children in particular are leaving notes and letters of 'Dear Santa' style in the hope that their dreams and wishes will be granted by the Little People.

The name and fame of Manannan has spread far, far wider than his cloak of mist could ever hope to. In April 1998, a crater discovered on Europa – that fascinating moon of the giant planet Jupiter – was named Manannan by the Harvard Smithsonian Institute of Astrophysics in Boston, USA. Europa is exciting astronomers because they believe it possible that beneath its frozen surface is a sea which could harbour life, water of course being the essential basic ingredient.

This moody and evocative photograph, looking south to the Sound along the island's west coast, is also interesting. In front of the Calf of Man can be seen what looks like the white stump of a broken lighthouse. Chicken Rock? Not quite. It is in fact another aid for the safe navigation of shipping in this treacherous area – Thousla Beacon, established on Thousla Rock in 1981. An octagonal concrete pillar standing in the Sound, it is easily seen from the nearby Sound Visitor Centre and cafe.

The Manx landscape is dotted with tholtans – the ruins of abandoned farmhouses or cottages, such as this at Killabrega, where there are wonderful views across the Sulby River. Tholtans were the homes of small-scale farmers (crofters) who for a long time represented a large proportion of the island's population.

The rural landscape as a whole, grazed by sheep and shaped by wind and weather, presents a picture of a past way of life which film makers find particularly refreshing in the search for such increasingly rare locations.

Add dramatic skies and seascapes to the equation and film makers are in seventh heaven!

Once you start digging there are endless mysteries to solve,

treasures to show off and bones to pick.

FIVE

Miss Marple investigates

It has never been made public, hence very few people are aware of it, but conspiracy theories abound on the Isle of Man. The only reason that this fact is not general knowledge is that it's been covered up. It makes sense.

Take, for example, the mysterious 11-day disappearance in December 1926 of the undisputed queen of crime, the brilliant (but possibly a little weird, touched as she was by genius) Agatha Christie.

It was a story which had the world's media baffled and bemused. There was absolutely no trace of her, and no clues to her whereabouts. Some reputable national newspapers even tried to recruit the services of Sherlock Holmes, but for reasons they never fathomed he ignored all their calls.

Eventually the truth was out: Agatha Christie's vanishing trick was nothing more than an unannounced get-away-from-it-all break in a Harrogate hotel – but *was* it the truth?

Was she, in fact, nowhere near Harrogate?

Was she, as the conspiracy theory goes, on the Isle of Man, sniffing out snuff and sewing the seeds of a dastardly plot to help the island's struggling hardware stores boost their sales of digging implements?

Indeed, did she have a card up her sleeve that was nothing less than the ace of spades itself?

And what would she have been doing on the Isle of Man so secretly, and incognito, in 1926?

The answer is looking for treasure. And there can be no doubt that she found it. Even in terms of inspiration alone, no one can dispute that the title *4.50 From Paddington* (one of her most famous whodunnits) sounds remarkably like 4.15 from Port Erin, and that the words *Murder On the Orient Express* roll off the tongue as easily as mudslide on the Manx Electric Railway. There's even a suggestion that Hercule Poirot was modelled on an island resident, maybe Harry Kelly of Cregneash.

True, Poirot wasn't educated enough to speak Manx Gaelic and presumably Harry wasn't exactly fluent in Flemish, but the names are similar.

So why was Agatha Christie looking for treasure? To satisfy her enquiring mind. That plus the fact that she was always up for a bit of digging – if not in the garden, Miss Marple style, then at the typewriter for storylines and plots.

And the idea of an ancient landscape packed to the rafters with the riches of peoples long since departed was just too compelling to pass up. She also knew that these riches were already being found.

The evidence was there from the work of noted antiquarians such as Philip Moore Callow Kermode and Lord Raglan, who between them had unearthed enough fascinating stuff to inspire the creation of the Manx Museum for the safekeeping and cataloguing of said items.

But, even in disguise, wouldn't she be conspicuous, shovelling big chunks out of the Manx landscape as she looked anxiously over her shoulder for the law? Of course not. On a popular seaside holiday island, what could be more innocent than carrying a bucket and spade

They seem strangely overdressed for work as strenuous as gathering in the harvest, but when history presents its case in photographic evidence, who can argue?

69

Top: In 1922, those people in favour of a national museum for the island saw their dream come true. Noble's Museum (so called because it was housed in a building vacated by Noble's Hospital, which had moved to a new site) opened on 2nd November on Crellin's Hill, Douglas, and attracted over 400 visitors in the first day – an encouraging start for curator Philip M.C. Kermode. Within months the name was changed to the Manx Museum.

Left middle: Imagine: St Patrick's Isle, on which stand the ruins of medieval Peel Castle and cathedral, was the site of the Holy Grail where King Arthur was crowned and Queen Guinevere buried. At least, this was the theory proposed in a book by an American professor who in 1986 came to see it all for himself. Some historians were not slow in declaring the idea utter tosh. So maybe it is true!

Salt of the earth

In 1891, believing that a coalfield extended across the Irish Sea from England, engineers drilled in the far north of the island. What coal was there did not present a viable commercial proposition, but something else did – the discovery by chance of a huge bed of salt, 5 square miles of it, beneath the sea, along with an underground river or lake of salt-rich brine. The Ramsey Salt Works subsequently exported table salt for millions of homes as well as salt for agricultural and manufacturing use. Customers included Russia! Obviously, the infamous salt mines of Siberia could not cope with domestic demand.

around with you? Agatha was no fool.

Two other real and well-documented events give even more credence to this particular conspiracy theory – and they both occurred in 1930.

First, Agatha Christie's obsession with all things buried (such as murder victims) was brought to the surface when, having divorced her first husband two years earlier, she married one Max Mallowan – an archaeologist so eminent that he went on to become Sir Max.

Second, she was asked by a Manx tourism committee to help bring in more visitors to the Isle of Man – a remarkably bold marketing initiative for the time, and a remarkable 'coincidence' that somebody should think of asking her of all people, after her secret 1926 visit.

Equally surprising, she agreed to do it, coming up with the idea of a treasure hunt for four gold snuff boxes, each containing a token for £100 (then, not to be sniffed at), buried somewhere in the Manx landscape.

The clues to their location lay in a story she wrote called *Manx Gold* which was serialised in the island's *Daily Dispatch*.

So the next question is why would a serious crime novelist agree to such a blatantly tacky commercial assignment?

For the money. That seems a good answer.

But a better answer is guilt. Having absconded from the island in 1926 with who knows what (maybe some priceless trinket from the unguarded grave of King Orry himself, or even

Far right below: Previously known as St Ninian, the roofless church of St Trinian stands on the main Douglas-Peel road. It dates from the 12th century and according to Manx folklore it is roofless because every attempt to complete the roof was foiled by a buggane – the evil hobgoblin of the Manx fairy kingdom. Inside the ruins are a number of cross slabs which originated from various places within the parish of Marown.

Right below: A listed historic monument in the care of Manx National Heritage, King Orry's Grave is located at Minorca (not the one in the Med – the one on the outskirts of Laxey) and the site is thought to be about 5,000 years old. The notion that the remains of King Orry are buried here is somewhat fanciful, as he is a mythical figure dating back to Viking times, which were far more recent. The other unusual feature of the grave (a long barrow) is that part of it lies in the garden of a private house. Mowing the lawn could be a bit on the spooky side!

The treasure's all mine!

- Finders are obliged to promptly report whatever they discover. If the Coroner then declares it treasure trove, the Manx Museum has first right to acquire it and the finder receives full market value.

- Fortune hunters who proved far less welcome on the Isle of Man were the predatory pickpockets who persistently mingled with summer holiday crowds. In 1933 such a thief came unstuck when his intended prey turned out to be a retired policeman. Fair cop, guv?

- In 1943, relics and skeletons were unearthed which were believed to date back to the Battle of Ronaldsway in 1275, when the leaderless Manx were overrun by the Scots in the name of Alexander III.

- The deepest digs have all been in the cause of mining – for lead, zinc, copper, tin, coal, oil, uranium and gold.

- In 1957 there were reports that oil had been discovered on the Isle of Man, but it turned out to be a hoax. However, in 1965 there was a controversial plan for an American company to build an oil refinery on the Ayres and to hunt for oil and natural gas in Manx waters. It sparked off a major conservation battle, ending in 1972 when the plan was scrapped.

- In 1968, divers discovered not a seahorse but a racehorse at the bottom of the sea! Did it come to grief at the waterjump and find itself in deeper trouble than expected? The facts rein in such a notion: it was the wreck of *HMS Racehorse*, a brig brought down in 1822 by the tricky rocks of Langness – a lethal hurdle for all shipping.

- One of the most remarkable finds of all was the discovery of *Peggy* – an 18th-century schooner-rigged yacht which was walled up in her boathouse in Castletown and was undiscovered for a century. On display in what is now the Nautical Museum, *Peggy* is officially listed as an historic ship by the National Maritime Museum in Greenwich.

the remains of King Orry – they can be very gruesome these crime writers), this was her way of easing a conscience plagued by nightmares of malevolent fairies and other dark creatures from Manx folklore. It all makes sense.

In 1966 another Isle of Man treasure hunt was employed to tempt tourists, this time with £3,000 in the chest. Cynics will already be thinking, "I bet whoever thought of that nicked it from 1930 but passed it off shamelessly as an original idea." Really? Do some people actually do that sort of thing?

If Agatha Christie *had* ransacked the Manx landscape in search of buried treasure, she couldn't have got away with too much because today there are riches for all to see, displayed in the Manx Museum in Douglas and at Manx National Heritage sites across the island. These sites all contribute to the telling of *The Story of Mann* and some are in truly stunning locations. Examples? The Sound Visitor Centre and cafe. The Meayll Circle – a Neolithic burial site. Lag ny Keeilley – a Manx keeill, a primitive form of church. Cronk ny Merriu – an Iron Age and later Norse promontory fort. The Niarbyl Visitor Centre and cafe. And there are more.

The treasures displayed in the Manx Museum include fine examples of Viking jewellery, some recovered from St Patrick's Isle, where the ruins of Peel Castle perch. Two of the biggest finds elsewhere are the Ballaquayle Hoard, discovered in the late 19th century, and a collection of coins, ingots and ornaments dug up in the area of Glenfaba, a sheading in which Tynwald Hill is

"You can have this very special luxury feed as long as you lay me a precious golden egg!"

What this lady at Harry Kelly's cottage in Cregneash didn't realise was that Cadbury's had already beaten them to it. In 1984 the great Cadbury egg treasure hunt was promoted across the UK. A dozen golden eggs, created and fashioned in 22-carat gold by the Crown jewellers Garrard and valued at £10,000 each, were buried at twelve different locations throughout the British Isles, one of them on the Isle of Man. Except that it wasn't the eggs which were buried but certificates of ownership, each one in a casket. Result? Pandemonium. Private land and places of Manx historic interest were thoughtlessly dug up all over the island. Cadbury's removed the casket, and the eventual winner, from England, identified the hiding place by post from a series of clues. The Manx egg was the last of the twelve to be won.

73

Maughold, close to Ramsey in the north-east of the island, is interesting for two main reasons: Maughold Head (with its breathtaking coastal views, fascinating birdlife and old lighthouse), and the cross house of Maughold churchyard (which displays fine examples of beautiful carved stone crosses, some of Celtic origin and others Norse).

located. The word sheading dates back to the time of the Vikings, who ran the island by dividing it into six parts.

The search for treasure still goes on, and will probably never end. There's a lot more out there. Another famous face who has joined in the fun is actor Tony Robinson – Baldrick of *Black Adder* fame. Tony and his TV *Time Team* spent three days poking their shovels into the past and they came up with a lost church, the body of a 6th-century woman and an inscribed slab of stone.

Working at a more sedate pace are those very patient people with headphones, slowly and silently hoovering Manx fields, oblivious to everything around them – except the exciting possibilities of what could lay beneath their feet. Metal detectors are very successful in prising secrets from the grip of the past and when they do it's a real buzz. Such was the case for two local islanders in 2008, who found part of a bronze decorated sword which dates back to about 900 AD and has created quite a stir. At the time of this book going to press the treasure was still being examined by archaeologists at Manx National Heritage, and in time it will be on permanent display in the Manx Museum's new Viking Gallery.

What would Agatha Christie or Miss Marple have given to uncover such secrets as this?

Cregneash village stands on the hillside overlooking the Sound and the Calf of Man. But it's not just this stunning location which makes it such an attraction. It's a living folk museum where traditional Manx crofting and farming skills are demonstrated in summer months. The village has also made a bit of a name for itself as a favourite film and TV location.

Up above the beautiful bay of Port Erin stands the mysterious Meayll (or Mull) Circle – a series of Neolithic burial chambers unique in the British Isles. Originally, as at Cashtal yn Ard, the stones and chambers would have been covered by a mound.

Right: Peel's haunted castle and cathedral ruins are more than a thousand years old and stand on St Patrick's Isle, alongside the harbour. The seven-acre site was occupied in Mesolithic and Iron Age times, and archaeological excavations have revealed items of great interest now displayed in the Manx Museum. At sunset the ruins cast a very evocative silhouette across the skyline. This alone is enough to motivate a visit to the nearby House of Manannan to see the equally thought-provoking presentation of Peel's past.

Far right: St Michael's chapel, or what is left of it, marks the isle of the same name at Derbyhaven and Langness. As far as is known, a buggane is not responsible for the absence of a roof.

When it comes to putting on a show, this place has

them rocking in the isles.

SIX

Break a leg

Is it really any wonder that the Isle of Man leads the world in entertainment? Think about it.

Where else could the expression 'break a leg' somehow take on extra meaning? What other place could be better suited for hosting rock concerts or providing an oasis for retiring rock legends than a bona fide, fully paid-up, music-loving, arts-loving rock? And when you consider some of the amazing acts which have appeared on this very steady rock's stages, the argument is signed, sealed, delivered and writing its acceptance speech ready to pick up the award.

One such act was Reg Rash, the pantomime horse. Having already tasted more than a fair share of fame and fortune in previous employment, he noticed one morning while trotting on the beach that the water looked particularly inviting. It was all the encouragement he needed to take the plunge and strike out for horizons new. The pack of seahorses he befriended en route were wide-eyed in awe as he told them of his astonishing track record: earnings approaching half a million pounds, father to 35 children, European Horse of the Year, and a record-breaker into the bargain. So engrossed was he in his own success story that before he knew it he'd ran out of sea and was shaking about 16 hands with a whole new adventure on a welcoming new land. And as the place he'd set out from was the Emerald Isle, Reg Rash reasoned rightly that this must be the Isle of Man.

Christmas audiences at the Gaiety Theatre in Douglas loved Reg Rash. They'd never seen a

You know you're in for a show as soon as you step inside the main entrance to the Villa Marina: all wood, marble, ironwork and bronze.

pantomime horse quite like this before. Forget two fat geezers stuffed inside a bit of stitched-up moth-eaten old curtain with a tail, they cried, we've got the real thing. And he was always very careful not to blow the gaff and disgrace himself on stage. Then, just as suddenly as he'd appeared on the scene, and not for the first time, Reg Rash vanished without trace. There was talk that he'd

Top: Stephen Fry starred in the TV hit *Tom Brown's Schooldays*, filmed at King William's College, Ronaldsway.

Above: Renee Zellweger and Ewan McGregor made for enjoyable viewing in *Miss Potter* – the acclaimed biopic of Beatrix Potter's own remarkable story, filmed in part on the Isle of Man.

Clips from the cutting room floor

- The expression 'break a leg' is a traditional verbal offering to someone about to perform on stage, and it arose from the superstition that to wish good luck is an open invitation for misfortune to do its worst instead.

- If you want to catch a Manx act that is unique in every detail and performed exclusively on the Isle of Man, don't miss Tynwald Day. All the legislative Acts passed during the last year are read out not only in English but in Manx Gaelic too. Fortunately, the remainder of the proceedings are a good deal more entertaining and the July event always draws a large crowd. In 1930 it reached an audience beyond the island's shores when it was broadcast by BBC radio.

- Isle of Man cinema audiences were first treated to the miracle of talking films in 1929. Twenty years later, an even bigger revolution arrived on the island – television!

- The Isle of Man's film industry began rolling in 1995, but the movie cameras had been on the island long before that. In 1928 shooting began for the screen adaptation of *Bondman* – a novel by Manx writer Sir Hall Caine, whose popularity was such that he achieved global book sales in excess of ten million.

- In 1935 another film unit arrived, along with film star Florence Desmond. Associated Talking Pictures were on the island to film an adaptation of a comedy by Walter Greenwood based on the TT. Another star, making his film debut, was Mr Ukulele himself, George Formby.

- Possible fame and fortune were among the incentives for the 175 girls who entered the 1936 Isle of Man Beauty Queen contest. The prize for the winner included a screen test at Ealing Studios.

- It simply isn't possible for every show and performance to go off in a blaze of glory – but unfortunately several Isle of Man entertainment venues have, destroyed or damaged by fire. They include Port Erin's Leslie's Pavilion, Onchan Head's Pavilion Theatre and Douglas's Strand Cinema. The latter was 1945 – the year in which the island's fire chief was preoccupied with being gaoled for stealing and selling ration books.

- On a happier note, despite the many tragedies suffered by island families in the Second World War, there was one loss which many Manx people and visitors were very happy about. This was in 1947, when dance band leader Joe Loss and his orchestra entertained appreciative and recovering audiences at the Villa Marina.

The gardens of the Villa Marina look across the promenade to Douglas Bay – the ideal night stage for an impressive pyrotechnics presentation.

Red and blue threaten to dominate in this colourful Gaiety Theatre
double bill on Douglas promenade.

fallen in with the TT crowd and the booze and burgers had piled on the pounds to such an extent that he'd joined those big beefy beasts that pulled the summer trams up and down Douglas prom.

And it was certainly common knowledge that the experimental new Express Service had failed because the round trip – up the prom and back, about 4 miles – was only taking 15 seconds and holidaymakers complained there wasn't time to enjoy the views or the ride. But after that? No trace. Reg Rash was never seen again.

And some have even commented that the name Reg Rash, rearranged, comes out as Shergar. The plot thickens.

Another entertaining but unlikely anecdote is the one about the Manx cat which (possibly smoking a cigar and being tended to by an entourage of eager porters) strode haughtily aboard an extremely posh 1930s Cunard liner at Liverpool. The ship was bound for New York but the cat was bound for California – and a glamorous new life with a Hollywood legend blessed with a great gift for elevating animals to silver screen stardom. It could only be Walt Disney. Walt, like many Americans before and since, obviously had a soft spot for the Isle of Man's most famous breed. For a cat with no tail, this one certainly had a big tale to tell. And best of all, it's a true story.

Then there was that huge carry-on in 1969 involving Ken, Sid and Hattie at the Regal Cinema in Douglas which attracted a big crowd and created world news. In front of everyone, the three of them were shamelessly loitering within tent and guilty of the most blatant inuendo as they fiddled with zips, grappled with ground rules and engaged in dubious goings-on after lights out. And they weren't the only ones at it. There was Charlie and Joan and Terry and Barbara too. Surely someone witnessing this outrageous behaviour called the *News of the World* for an exclusive? No need. It was all in good fun – the world premiere of *Carry On Camping*, attended in person by the since departed Hattie Jacques, Kenneth Williams and Sid James.

The Regal Cinema has gone too, demolished in 1983. With it went the world's earliest surviving facade created (in 1888) by renowned Victorian theatre architect Frank Matcham, who a decade later returned to the Isle of Man to work his magic in and on the Gaiety Theatre. Before conversion to a cinema, the Regal was the Grand Theatre.

Forty years prior to the carry-on at the Regal, a much greater one was coming to a head along Douglas promenade and Strand Street. It was also in the name of entertainment but, for many people, and particularly shopkeepers, fun wasn't quite the word it brought to mind. In the 1920s the Isle of Man was really packing in visitors in big numbers. Publishers of sheet music were well in tune with the golden opportunity such a mass audience presented, promoting their latest songs from street booths manned by singers. The booths were not classed as entertainment and did not require a licence so it was a free for all.

Success breeds greed and the booths bit the

By Royal Hall command at the Villa Marina: Elkie Brooks in concert.

Douglas's other popular marina, where putting on a show and topping the bill mean something different altogether.

Out on the town – Castle Street, Douglas. 89

Right: **The painstaking and successful restoration of the Gaiety Theatre was all about attention to fine detail, being faithful to the original work of Frank Matcham and a refusal to compromise. 'Officially' the restoration took 10 years but in fact the work had started long before the campaign to complete it in time for the theatre's centenary in 2000 actually kicked off.**

The restored canopy boasts lots of stained glass.

Middle: **The upper facade, now good as new, was in particularly desperate need of a facelift.**

dust and large open-fronted singing halls sprang up – an even bigger attraction when the weather wasn't too good. Now the singers had a pianist and everyone was invited and cajoled into joining in the chorus. A jolly time was had by all – except those people who were inconvenienced and annoyed by the congestion and sometimes unbearable noise caused by these Strand Street halls. Other businesses and shops in the street were understandably miffed. For one thing, potential customers who couldn't stand the racket were rushing by instead of calling in to browse and buy. For another, the problem was

compounded by the invasion of the Tommy Talkers – a toy-like trumpet you could buy anywhere and which was absolutely guaranteed to further blow the minds and eardrums of those already driven to the brink of a breakdown.

And did the thousands of good-time holidaymakers who loved nothing more than to sing and dance in the streets till long after dark give a monkey's about such sensitivities? In a word, no.

In fact, the Isle of Man is long renowned for its prowess and popularity in the singing department. In 1932, a record crowd of 13,000

people packed into the Manx Highland Gathering – more than a quarter of the island's population according to the 1931 census. The singing voice of guest Sir Harry Lauder was one of the big attractions.

A particularly momentous year in the history of Manx entertainment was 1964. Commercial pirate station Radio Caroline North created more than a few waves by anchoring itself in Ramsey Bay. Manx Radio broadcast its voice for the first time, covering the TT. And the rising Rolling Stones performed live for one night at Douglas's Palace Ballroom. There was plenty of screaming from adoring fans, but no dancing – the audience of 12,000 were crammed in tighter than sardines!

A similar show of applause, excitement and sheer joy – but on a vastly greater scale and by a far smaller audience – was released at the Gaiety Theatre on 8th May 1945 during the Manx Music Festival. The show was halted so that the audience could listen live to an historic event in world broadcasting history: the address to the British nation by Prime Minister Winston Churchill that the Germans had surrendered and the war was over.

And this is also a true story.

91

Pirates? No – tall ships which sailed into Douglas for the 2007 centenary TT, though not to compete.

Left: More aspects of the Gaiety's acclaimed new (but old) face. When Brian Matcham (the great nephew of Frank) paid a surprise visit to the theatre in 1998, he was overcome by the experience. "If the old man walked in now," he said, "he would find it exactly as it was on the last day that he saw it."

Left below: And more fireworks lighting up the Irish Sea – this time over Port Erin.

Douglas has many fine
restaurants – not really
surprising when you consider
the island's remarkable growth
in recent years as an important
and attractive offshore finance
centre. Variety is the spice of
eating out, with international
cuisine competing against local
fresh seafood.

Pubs are another popular option – but proprietors prefer any fireworks to be of the strictly pyrotechnic variety, and well out of harm's way!

The only place in the English-speaking world

with twenty-seven letters in the alphabet

– because there's not just one T but two.

An extraordinary island race

On the subject of Manx entertainment and playing to huge audiences, you could never be taken seriously if you didn't include the Isle of Man TT.

According to its well-documented history, this unique road racing spectacle was kick-started in 1904 by a few cars competing in trials. Motorbikes roared on to the scene three years later and that's when the action really took off, as celebrated by the TT's big centenary in 2007.

It was an unbearable intrusion, and the Little People (also known to the Manx as Themselves) resigned themselves to packing their bags. But they didn't head for Douglas or the fairy terminal. They didn't even travel overland. Their destination was underground – deep in the bowels of the island, where even Agatha Christie's dubious diggings wouldn't be able to reach them.

And as they made their descent into inner peace, they generously gifted a curse on the

 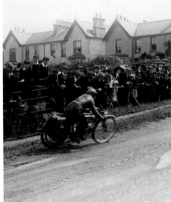 

Far left: 1914: riders setting off at the top of Bray Hill to start the Junior race.

Middle: 1912/13: Australian rider Les Bailey at Cruickshanks Corner, May Hill, Ramsey.

Left: 1911: Harry Collier, crossing Ballig Bridge (as opposed to Fairy Bridge), looks very determined – determined to annoy the Little People maybe.

So much for history. But there are those who point to an altogether different series of events as the real reason for the birth of the TT – and it's all deeply rooted in Manx folklore.

If there was one thing the Little People felt threatened by, and detested, it was large – especially as in large numbers of Victorian holidaymakers turning up by the boatload and trampling all over Mother Nature's delicate Manx countryside with their size twelves and screaming kids.

island's humankind.

"If you want noise and chaos and mayhem, you can have it – big time and for ever and with knobs on. And don't get thinking that waving to us from that stupid bridge will get you anywhere, because it won't."

This was their solemn promise – and they delivered. Say hello to the TT.

Now whether or not you believe in such airy fairy folklore, you have to acknowledge that the TT does annoy an awful lot of people, especially

97

Who dares, wins. Motorcycle racers know the risks – but it doesn't lessen the tragedy when the sport loses one of its stars. Robert Dunlop was fatally injured in a race event off island in 2008.

amongst the island's resident population.

They constantly voice such gripes as the traffic and ferry mayhem caused by the annual invasion of bikers, the inconvenience to shopping because of the road closures and empty shelves, and the conviction that racing on two wheels at speeds of up to 200 miles an hour on roads that were never built for it is sheer madness and no other nation or place on the planet would entertain it. How Themselves must be laughing their little socks off at creating such misery and argument. Revenge!

On the other side of the TT coin (and quite a few have been minted over the years), what Themselves hadn't bargained for was the sheer raw excitement and all the thrills, spills, skills and ringing tills that would spin off their curse, making lots of humankind very happy in the process. Happy was definitely not part of the plan. You can bet your bottom dollar that Mother Nature has never been so miffed.

And what makes the survival of the TT so extraordinary is that despite the many obstacles it has had to endure and overcome during its long life – from political pressures and courting controversy to finding the funding and calls for its closure – this truly unique event is still at the races. The folklore may be bogus but perhaps some other higher authority has ordained that the TT was and is simply meant to be.

TT fortnight comprises a week of practice followed by the big event – a spectacle of hair-raising racing and fun-filled festival. The whole show gets on the road in late May but the preparation never stops. Like clockwork, as the spring bank holiday approaches, the TT experience, metaphorically speaking, is rolled out of the garage, wiped down with a damp sponge and an oily rag, and let loose on the Mountain Course, completely dominating island life. Even when the action is all over and the 40,000 or so fulfilled fans have gone home to shed the effects of too much drinking, feasting, partying and other excesses, the TT is never silent on the Isle of Man. And it is, in every sense, a lesson for survival.

Despite casting their malevolent spell before going underground, Themselves were not above a bit of sport. In fact they had a particular liking for riding horses. But it wouldn't be fair to saddle them with any blame for what happened in 1902 at a summer horse race meeting near Douglas. A thousand paying customers packed into the venue, looking forward to a good day's racing and, as ever, optimistic of picking up a quid or two along the way. But the four-legged racers on whom all punters' hopes were pinned weren't quite so keen on the idea.

Only two of them had bothered to throw off their horse blankets, drag themselves out of the

2007: the centenary TT in full swing behind the scenes as attention focuses on the leaderboard, pits, race control, marshalling, timekeeping, technical checking...

101

Top: 1963 Senior: John Hartle at Governor's Bridge in the race won by Mike Hailwood.

Above: 1998: Happier times for the Dunlop family. Joey and younger brother Robert before the 125cc race, which Robert won.

TT Trivia

- In the 1920s, some Manx business leaders expressed the fear that the TT was a deterrent to well-heeled visitors and the island's tourism was losing out to Blackpool and other resorts.

- In 1946 two 'lost' TT trophies awarded in 1939 were found, one in Germany, one in Italy.

- The slowest ever lap of the TT course was completed in 1998. It took eleven and a half hours – a truly awesome feat when you consider that it was performed by a one-legged ex-policeman in a wheelchair! Swazie Turner did it all in the good cause of raising money for cancer research.

- The 1939 Senior TT was won by German Georg Meier on a BMW but his presence in the race caused a lot of unease.

- For the TT's 2007 centenary, Isle of Man Post Office created a set of 10 stamps featuring the fans' choice of all-time greats: Stanley Woods, Geoff Duke, Bob McIntyre, Giacomo Agostini, Mike Hailwood, Steve Hislop, Joey Dunlop, David Jefferies, Dave Monlyneux and John McGuinness.

- Unlucky number 13 was dropped from the TT in 1937 but has been used again in recent years.

- Barry Sheene won two 500cc world championships but gave up on TT racing at the first attempt, in 1971.

- At the 1914 TT, armed guards with bayonets were posted outside the marquee where bikes were kept overnight. This was because of fears that the Suffragette movement, very active at the time, could decide to cause trouble.

- The idea of kick-starting bikes was pioneered by Eric Myers, who used the method to start his machine for the 1909 TT. It was not until the 1960s that electric starting became the norm.

- The highest number of TT victories achieved by any rider is 26. Irishman Joey Dunlop, MBE, OBE, chalked up these wins between 1976 and 2000. The Joey Dunlop Foundation was set up in his memory, primarily as a charity to aid injured riders.

- The record for the highest number of sidecar TT wins (11) is held by Manx native and resident Dave Molyneux.

- The TT circuit, 37.73 miles long, is known as the Mountain Course because a section of it skirts around Snaefell, the highest peak on the Isle of Man. There are more than 225 corners and the course crosses 6 rivers.

Top left: **Preparing the course: repainting kerbside high-visibility stripes.**

Top middle: **"Anybody seen my motorbike anywhere?"**

Top right and left: **The chequered flag – a sight familiar to 11-times TT winner John McGuinness.**

Far right: Fabulous fireworks, gorgeous girls and singing policemen all add to the spectacle, good humour and party atmosphere – not exactly what the Little People had in mind!

stable and turn up for work. The proprietor then chucked a further hurdle into the ring by refusing to refund admission money. Obviously, a gambling man.

Back on the TT scene, in pre-bikes 1906 the car race winner was a certain Charles Rolls. He not only won the 160-mile race but kindly obliged the statisticians by doing so in a fraction over 4 hours, making the calculation of his average speed a doddle. And naturally, the car he was driving was one of his own making – a Rolls-Royce.

Although being displaced in TT terms by motorcyles, cars have made their racing mark on the Isle of Man in a variety of ways over quite a few decades. In summer 1933, Douglas introduced street racing, which was already a familiar sight in Monte Carlo. Two 50-lap races provided plenty of excitement for spectators, including a spattering of crashes. Winner of one race was TT star Freddie Dixon, who was physically strong and had a reputation for being a bit of a hooligan – not the sort of bloke to be bothered by Themselves.

In the following year, a practice run for the same race resulted in the death of a young mechanic, thrown from the MG driven by Kaye Don, a famous name in British motorsport. Don was badly injured but found guilty of manslaughter and gaoled for four months. Despite this the races were declared a great success.

The TT course was back in the news again in 1936, hosting the first Manx International Bicycle Race for amateurs. The winner completed the one-lap 37.73 miles race at an average speed of 22 miles an hour.

But by this time the Isle of Man's real sporting high fliers were up, up and away – not in balloons but aircraft. A sort of round-island two-lap race of 108 miles excited crowds in 1932, even though one of the pilots was so low coming in to land that she fractured the thigh of a spectator sitting on a hedge! The idea of air racing really took off from here, with a London to Isle of Man air race in 1936 and a Manx Air Derby in 1937, repeated in 1938 and 1939. At the latter, a Messerschmitt with a German pilot was conspicuous by its absence – withdrawn from entry because, with war clouds gathered over Europe once again, Luftwaffe commander Reichmarshall Goering refused to give his permission.

No such authorisation was ever needed for two other notorious high-speed races on the Isle of Man – the tidal race currents which rip through the channels of the Ayres in the extreme north and the Sound in the extreme south. They're pretty wild places. In fact, they're pretty *and* wild – a million miles from the TT and just the sort of beauty spots nature-made to slow you down so that you can appreciate the peace, tranquillity and wildlife.

Even the foulest of Little People would find it hard to stay grumpy surrounded by this kind of magic.

Right top: **1950: Kate's Cottage,** one of the best-known landmarks of the **TT course,** with spectators in vantage points they wouldn't be allowed to occupy today.

Right bottom: **1933: Tommy Spann** on the infamous and hair-raising **Bray Hill descent.**

Far right: **Joey Dunlop** doing his stuff at **Ballaugh Bridge.**

Other racing and sporting highlights

- The Isle of Man's first Sportsman of the Year (1953) was a woman – acclaimed international cyclist Millie Robinson.

- The 1937 London-Isle of Man air race was won by a German pilot in a Messerschmitt, the tail fin of which bore the swastika of Nazi Germany.

- In 1930, a 100-mile round-island swim of the Isle of Man took Miss Mercedes Gleitze, who had already notched up a swim across the English Channel, a gruelling 56 hours 45 minutes.

- The Parish Walk, now a challenge featuring on the Manx events calendar, was conceived in 1923. It took island politician Gerald Bridson MHK (Member of the House of Keys) 20 hours 23 minutes to walk 80 miles touching the door of all 17 of the Isle of Man's parish churches.

- In 1962, Beryl Swain from London became the first woman to compete in a solo class of the TT.

- In 2000, the Isle of Man took on the world – in the BT Global Challenge Round The World Yacht Race.

Don't try a stunt like this in the High Street – but it's okay for Isle of Man-based trials star Steve Colley, who doesn't seem to mind that there's a wheel missing!

111

A land of weird questions, strange answers, giants,

Little People and bounty hunters.

EIGHT

Creatures real and imagined

There are plenty of hairy beasts running wild on the Isle of Man – and not just bikers. And if the island isn't the perfect place to let your imagination do the same, where is?

All you have to do is find a suitably quiet spot, close your eyes and open your mind. The Sound, the Ayres, a wooded glen, the summit of Snaefell – the wilder the better. And don't worry about the inescapable feeling that you're being watched. You are (but the police are bound to catch him eventually). The fear will vanish into thin but very fresh air as soon as your imagination kicks in and those intensely challenging questions start prodding you for answers. Are you ready?

Is it a coincidence that UFO has three letters? Does it imply some special affinity with the Isle of Man? It's certainly the ideal place to look up to the possibility. Big skies, very little light pollution, broad horizons and a largely rural landscape: little wonder there have been numerous strange and unexplained sightings over the years. Focus binoculars on a clear night sky and you'll be astonished at the universe revealed to you. The star-packed Milky Way can look as solid as the Irish Sea.

Thoughts of the bigger picture raise another big question: could the Isle of Man's very convenient position slap bang in the middle of the north Irish Sea mean that it was a stepping stone for giants to hop between Ireland, England, Wales and Scotland as the fancy took them? Was it put there by the giant of County Antrim's causeway fame? Or by early ancestors of the Isle of Man's very own Sulby giant?

Are those wallabies who wander free in the Curraghs the result of the secret exchange scheme whereby the British Isles sent convicts and other unwashed to Oz and received something in return?

Who originally decided to pull the tails off Manx cats? The evil Black Dog of Peel Castle? Or was it the handy work of some other mischievous entity from Manx folklore – a bored buggane or a fed-up phynodderee? Or is there a much simpler explanation? Did Manx cats of old have a particularly abrasive tongue which inadvertently destroyed their own tails in the act of performing ablutions?

And was it that same abrasive tongue, expressed offensively, which drove the Black Dog barking mad and initiated the whole dog-hate-cat scenario exploited so comically by Disney and other animators?

Do people of a nervous disposition but brave enough to climb to the high viewing platform at the top of the Laxey Wheel have a point in referring to it as the Laxative Wheel?

Is the Fairy Bridge a bad case of inappropriate labelling? Manx folklore makes no bones about the beings in question cringing with horror at being likened to wand-waving ballerinas with gossamer wings. Such an elementary mistake. The mind boggles.

And as it does, maybe you will be struck by the biggest and most profound question of all: is the name Isle of Man not only sexist but species-ist? Here in the liberated and enlightened 21st century, shouldn't Tynwald be putting aside such

There's nothing imaginary about the pleasure steamer *Balmoral*, which is a regular annual visitor to the Isle of Man and seen here off St Patrick's Isle, Peel.

113

Far left: Does a mighty giant lie sleeping beneath mighty Castle Rushen?

Middle: If it was a wheel on a mountain bike, Laxey's giant would make such a bike big enough to tackle Everest!

Left: One of the biggest swings in the world? Ramsey harbour's iron swingbridge.

Big on giants

- Langness is an ornithologists' paradise, rich in birdlife all year round. But in 1925 a much bigger visitor was the centre of attention. A dead female sei whale, 48 feet (14.63 m) long, 7 feet (2.13 m) high and weighing an estimated 40 tons, was washed up on the peninsula. It took the power of two traction engines to transport the deceased to Douglas. Since 1937 the skeleton has been on display in the Manx Museum.

- Another story which made massive news was that of the Sulby Giant – James Arthur Caley (1824-1889), the biggest Manxman on record. At the age of 22 he was already 7 feet 6 inches (2.29 m) tall and weighed in at 21 stones (648 kg), allegedly increasing to 8 feet (2.44 m) and 44 stones (1358 kg). He left the Isle of Man for North America to join Barnum and Bailey's Circus, in which he was known by the name of Colonel Ruth Goshon – an odd choice considering there is no record of his ever having had a sex change. He is remembered in the Manx Museum through photographs, a pair of his boots and a cast of his enormous hands.

- The statistics of the restored Great Laxey Wheel, one of the biggest ever constructed in the world, make it a giant even by the standards of Victorian engineering. Diameter: 72 feet (22 m). Circumference: 228 feet (69.4 m). Breadth: 6 feet (1.8 m). Number of water buckets: 168. Bucket capacity: 24 gallons (109 litres). Every minute it could raise 250 gallons (1,136 litres) of water through a height of 1500 feet (457 m). The wheel is in the care of Manx National Heritage.

- Not quite in the same league but making big news during the Second World War was the 18-ton flywheel (subsequently nicknamed the Kelly Bug, as in Doodlebug) which ran out of control at Douglas Power Station and created havoc. Its sectional rim disintegrated, shooting parts through the roof and a thousand feet into the air, one piece crashing through the roof of Douglas Gas Works on its descent. Another piece hit a house, trapping two women in the debris. Amazingly, no one was injured in the incident but it left the entire island without power, for up to 14 hours in some places.

- According to Manx folklore, beneath Castle Rushen lie miles of underground passages, chambers and a magnificent mansion in which a giant sleeps on a table. Wake him and you'll never see daylight again. Does this terrifying secret explain why only 4% of the island's population now lives in the town which for centuries was the capital of the Isle of Man?

A real invasion or a trick of the light? Relax. It's a Viking re-enactment at Peel.

The dead sei whale which was washed up on the Langness peninsular in 1925. Two traction engines were needed to transport the 40-ton bulk to Douglas, where the bones were stripped so that the enormous skeleton could be displayed in the Manx Museum.

mundane matters as budgets and law and order and economic policy, and debating instead the crucially important question of whether the island should at last recognise the urgent need to rename itself the Isle of Persons And Animals? The PC brigade are up for it big time, so it must be right.

The generous commission from Ordnance Survey and other cartographers for all the map and atlas reprint business could be used to fund another equally brilliant PC project. Or at least, lots of meetings to arrange further meetings to discuss the possibility of talking about the idea at some future date to be pencilled in if and when a window becomes available or a door becomes unhinged.

On slipping into this very dark abyss you suddenly realise that you've dozed off and become entwined in a hellish nightmare. For one heart-stopping moment you think your holiday is over and you are back in chains, your boss standing over you accusingly. So just take a deep breath and remember the excellent advice in *The Hitch-Hiker's Guide to the Galaxy*: don't panic.

Now open your eyes and look around you. The landscape, a picture of myth, legend and superstition, is reassuringly beautiful, and there's no missing the abundance and variety of wildlife which enriches land, air and sea – the inspiration for the odd incredible creature tale or two.

Take that story of dogs heavily into drugs. Saturday night binge drinkers popping pills? No. Further investigation revealed them to be police sniffer dogs. Then there was the wallaby caught

in 1994 at Ramsey Hairpin, a famous feature of the TT course. How exciting! Was he or she by any chance speeding on a stolen motorbike? No. Just going about the business of being one of the wild wallabies which have lived free on the Isle of Man for several decades, descendants of escapees from Curraghs Wildlife Park. So what about the big cat discovered at Port Soderick – surely an exotic Bengal tiger or rare snow leopard fallen from a passing aircraft? Another disappointment: merely the launch of the world's biggest ocean-going catamaran, built on the Isle of Man. Then there was the mad dash to catch the crocodile in the new Summerland cinema. Foiled again: the screening of *Crocodile Dundee 2*. So it obviously goes without saying that the highly unlikely report of bounty hunters putting rabbits on the

run is yet another attempt at a sensational headline covering a mundane story?

No! This one is true. In 1985, to curb the increasing number of rabbits hopping destructively all over the island, Tynwald introduced bounty payments – bunny money for every genuine rabbit's bobtail removed from its deceased owner and handed in to an official collector.

Well over a quarter of a million tails registered a claim for cash – until allegations of abuse of this hare-brained scheme revealed scams such as importing tails from rabbits caught in the UK, recycling tails that had already been paid for and, cheekiest of all, submitting bobs that were nothing more than bits of old teddy bear – proof that some people will do anything for a

Sulby Glen is a true beauty spot, nestling below the slopes of Snaefell and running through a narrow valley. Nearby is Sulby Reservoir, which was completed in 1983 and holds 1,000 million gallons of water – quite a lot by any standards. The Sulby River – the longest on the island – flows through the glen on its way to the sea at Ramsey.

117

If you want time and space to sit back, relax and let your imagination run riot, there's no more amenable location than beautiful Port Erin.

quick buck.

Not that bounty hunting was anything new on the Isle of Man. Long before the Manx equivalent of Clint Eastwood and Lee Van Cleef rode into town for rabbit trophies, you could earn a few bob similarly separating tails of a more impressive length from another pest – that unmentionable three-lettered rodent which for centuries superstition has associated with bad luck. The money gave the challenge an extra edge and it was attacked with relish, continuing until 1966 and paying out four old pence per tail. So if you handed in three tails (a rat-trick?) you'd pick up the princely sum now equivalent to five pence. But then Tynwald spoiled all the fun by dropping the bounty and pinning its money on poison. This naturally upset birds of prey. Fearing contamination of the food chain, they had to live up to their name – offer a prayer to the great bird in the sky in the hope that their next tasty Roland or two wouldn't prove to be their last supper.

It needed more than prayers to fight the lost cause of trying to save the population of female dog whelks in Port St Mary harbour in 1990. They suffered atrocious mutations at the hands of dangerous chemicals released by boat anti-fouling paint, causing them to explode under the pressure of being unable to lay their eggs – a gruesome end which stand-up comics, merciless as ever, quickly likened to the title of David Frost's groundbreaking TV satire of the 1960s with the quip, "That was the whelk that was."

A few years later, a Manx fisherman had better

There's plenty of time and space to chew things over above Port Erin Bay.

Animal snaps

- Horses are a common sight on the Isle of Man – working the land at Cregneash, carrying riders through the countryside, hauling the trams along Douglas promenade in summer and, until 1970, pulling milk floats. At the end of their working lives the tram horses take it easy in their dedicated retirement home – an improvement on the past policy of selling them for pet food! In the Victorian boom era, the trams were carrying more than 1.75 million passengers a year.

- At various times since opening, Curraghs Wildlife Park has brought many interesting animals to the island. They include a baby elephant from Burma, sea lions from Peru (which of course is where Paddington Bear hails from, although he has never been to the park), lion cubs, bear cubs, a variety of monkeys, ring-tailed lemurs, flamingos, tropical birds and endangered wetland species of birds and animals from around the world.

- Animal escape stories include wallabies from Curraghs Wildlife Park (and now established in the wild), baboons from a show in Onchan and a large monkey from a show at the original Camera Obscura in Douglas.

- Over a three-year period in the 1970s, a very sociable and easily-identifiable dolphin who came to be known as Donald was a regular Isle of Man visitor. He befriended many local divers in Port Erin, Port St Mary and Derbyhaven and even let one female diver ride astride him. But not everyone was keen on his presence and he suffered shotgun wounds and the threat of being put down. Other adventures included rescue when he was stranded in tidal mud. Donald finally departed in 1973 when explosives were being used to carry out improvements in Port St Mary harbour.

luck when he too found himself in an explosive situation. He landed a catch six feet long and weighing 500 pounds, but his bubble of excitement burst when he realised it was old

ending Manx storybook, such as the defeated proposal for holidaymakers to hunt basking sharks.

As for the elusive creatures of Manx folklore

Above: Loaghtan sheep, a native Manx breed, can have up to six horns.

Above right: Endangered ring-tailed lemurs can be seen in the protected environment of Curraghs Wildlife Park.

ordnance – a torpedo-shaped bomb. The Royal Navy's disposal squad quickly put the dampers on any possibility of the situation blowing up in their faces by detonating it safely underwater.

There are plenty more animal and wildlife-related tales to tell from the pages of the never-

and visiting UFOs, the ever-dependable cynics have a simple explanation: it's all in the very vivid imaginations of those people with vested interests in boosting the Isle of Man's tourism industry.

As if!

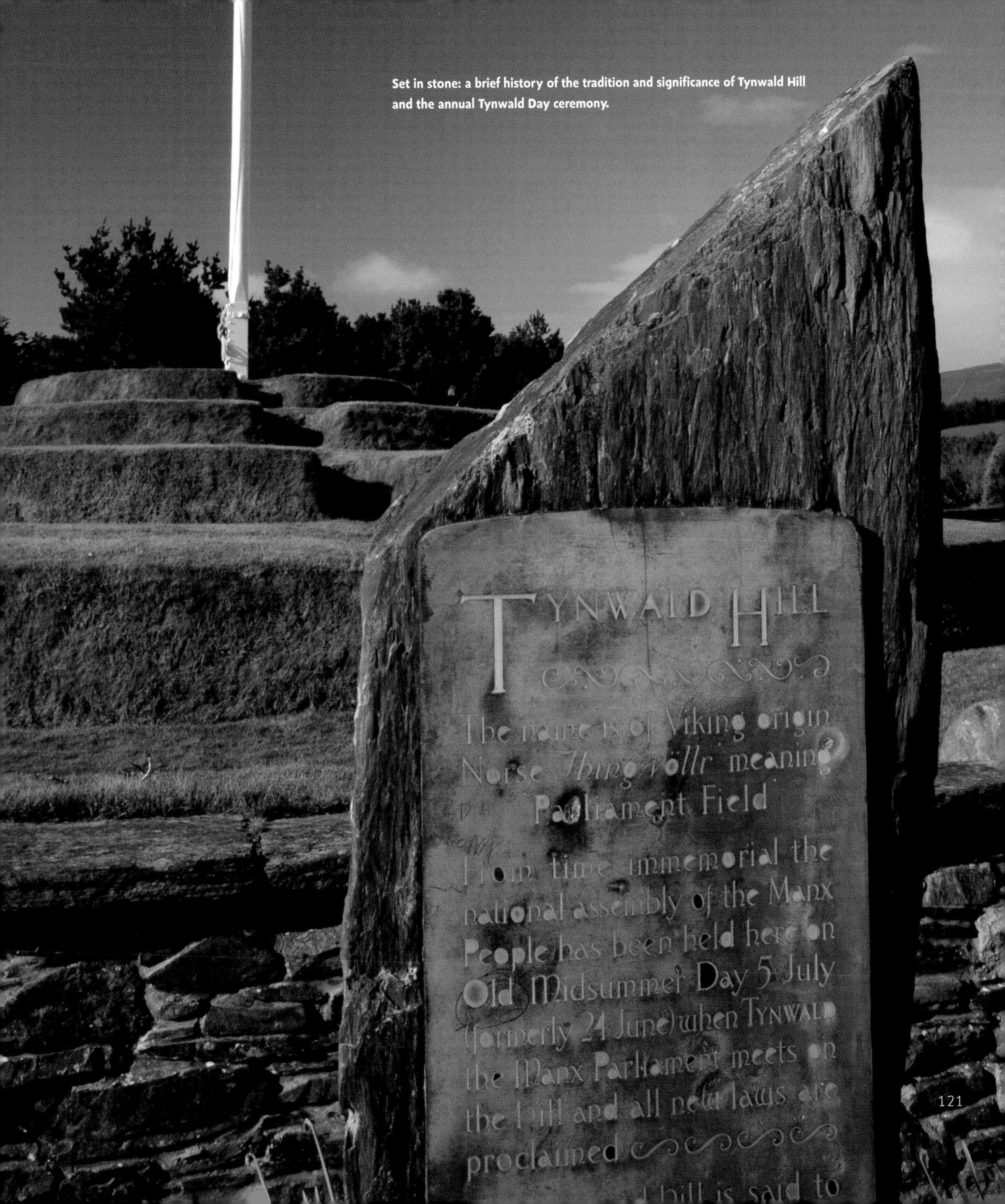

Set in stone: a brief history of the tradition and significance of Tynwald Hill and the annual Tynwald Day ceremony.

TYNWALD HILL

The name is of Viking origin
Norse *Thing völlr* meaning
Parliament Field

From time immemorial the
national assembly of the Manx
People has been held here on
Old Midsummer Day 5 July
(formerly 24 June) when Tynwald
the Manx Parliament meets on
the hill and all new laws are
proclaimed

hill is said to

Garwick Bay, near Laxey on the east coast. Is that merely a storm cloud gathering? A buggane brewing up trouble? The mischief of malevolent Little People in the making? And dare you risk hanging around long enough to find out?

Right: Seen from a distance, the Great Laxey Wheel doesn't seem such a big shot – but get closer and you'll realise you spoke too soon!

Below left: Little tern favour the pebbly beaches of the Ayres, which also support good breeding populations of oystercatcher and ringed plover.

Below right: It's a typical Manx paradox that the island's common seals are far less common than the Atlantic grey seals – by a ratio of something like ten to one!

Top photos: The Manx countryside is green, idyllic and invites exploration. But beware of fairy mounds and music – you could be taken by the Little People and never seen again. Or so the superstition goes.

Below: Winter snow on the Isle of Man doesn't always look so pretty. In the snowstorm of 1929, for example, school buses were stranded in drifts 15 feet deep. Children who couldn't get home to remoter parts of the island had to be put up overnight in any house that would take them.

If you're ever out on the town on the Isle of Man and a party of

seafarers invite you to tag along and get wrecked, beware.

Don't let Saturday night exuberance carry you overboard.

It won't necessarily be the whisky that's on the rocks.

NINE

Man the lifeboats

Where in the world could anybody at sea be safer than the waters around the Isle of Man? Isn't this the very place where Sir William Hillary famously came up with his most celebrated and miraculous invention ever – the lifeboat?

No. This is a complete but common misconception. But on the other hand yes. It's quite close to the truth. Sort of. If you stretch a point or two.

was the vision and driving force behind the formation, in 1824, of the National Institution for the Preservation of Life from Shipwreck, later renamed the Royal National Lifeboat Institution.

So after all that, if Sir William Hillary didn't invent the lifeboat, who did? For the answer you have to dive a little further back into the ever-murky and muddled depths of history.

The earliest written record in Britain of a boat dedicated specifically to saving lives takes you to

The Ramsey lifeboat, slip sliding away. They don't launch 'em like this any more!

William Hillary was a man of many parts but inventor wasn't one of them. He frequently risked his life in lifeboats but didn't design or build a single one. He helped save more than three hundred people from drowning but couldn't swim. He lived in Douglas, a baronet and a hero, but died miserably and alone. And he

Formby in Lancashire in 1777. This is both confirmed, yet typically contradicted, by records which suggest that there was a pre-RNLI lifeboat station at Formby before there was a boat – in 1776, in fact. But hey, nothing wrong with being prepared. And the notion "let's build a lifeboat station in case somebody ever invents a lifeboat"

127

Built for speed – today's Ramsey lifeboat and the Steam Packet's fastcraft monohull *Viking*.

is not really so crazy, is it?

After all, there was certainly a need for such a sea ambulance, and an increasingly dire need at that. During the mad maritime era of the 18th century, vessels were going down like flies, not least because shipping lanes serving busy ports such as Cardiff, Dublin, Glasgow and Liverpool were swarming with them. It was crazier than Spaghetti Junction in the crush hour. The equivalent of the hard shoulder must have been littered with the spoils of bumps and scrapes: ripped rigging, kinked keels and no end of worse-for-wear anchors.

Adding to the tailbacks would have been scores of warships. And all at the mercy of the weather – such as those naval vessels which suffered a mighty blow in 1703, wrecked in the Great Storm off the coast of Kent. In boating terms this corner of south-east England is a bit of a pull from the Irish Sea – but it just happens to be the very county in which lies a clue to answering the question about who really invented lifeboats. It's an inscription on the grave of a man called Lionel Lukin, describing him as the first to build such a boat. How thoughtful of whichever family member it was who added this detail, knowing that one day (and even the day after) somebody somewhere would want to know. So: the truth at last. Mystery solved!

Don't be silly – this is history we're talking about. You just know that it can't be this simple. If it was, some mischievous academic, fearful of being out of a job, would surely contrive to turn the trail into a big bag of worms all tangled up

Chicken Rock lighthouse was built by the famous Stevenson family (of *Treasure Island* connection) and became operational on 1st January 1875. Almost 86 years later to the day, it made worldwide news when fire broke out in the tower and it took great courage and ingenuity by the lifeboats of Port St Mary and Port Erin to rescue the three stranded duty keepers. The lighthouse was repaired and is still operating – solar powered and unmanned.

Written in the stars?

The omens were there: that bad luck would at some time strike was always on the cards for Chicken Rock lighthouse.

First came the decision by Commissioners of Northern Lighthouses to relocate the shore station for the lighthouse from the Calf of Man, the home of two earlier lighthouses, to Port St Mary. This happened in 1875. Their reason? On visiting the Calf they discovered that the only other inhabitant was a farmer, and he was unable to grow any fresh produce to supply to the Chicken Rock keepers because his gardens were completely overrun – by those dreaded long-tailed rodents which Manx superstition insists are carriers of ill fortune.

The second omen? In order to build the lighthouse it was necessary to cut, shape and number the blocks of Scottish granite quarried for the purpose. A project base was established at Port St Mary, less than 5 miles from Chicken Rock, where the craftsmen could carry out this work. And the name of the tug which would tow the assembly-ready blocks by sea to Chicken Rock? *Terrible*.

The Calf of Man and Chicken Rock lighthouse also have unlikely literary connections, though not with each other.

In 1937, after many years in private ownership, the Calf of Man was placed in the care of the National Trust for Places of Historic Interest and Natural Beauty by an anonymous benefactor. It transpired that the donor was a Mr F.J. Dickens of Lancashire – a man with Manx connections and a descendant of Charles Dickens.

Chicken Rock lighthouse is the creation of the remarkable family of Scottish engineers, the Stevensons. More specifically, the brothers David and Thomas Stevenson, Thomas being the first engineer of the Northern Lighthouse Board and also father to no less a storyteller than Robert Louis (pronounced Lewis) Stevenson – author of *Treasure Island*, the enduring popularity of which is such that it has never been out of print since it was published in 1883. It was originally entitled *The Sea-Cook* and before appearing as a novel was serialised in a magazine.

And is there a story in why Chicken Rock is so called? Of course. It's all because of the storm petrel – a black and white bird which resembles a swallow but is closely related to the fulmar and shearwater and was known to sailors as Mother Carey's chicken. When ornithologists discovered that the rocky reef was a popular perching place for these birds, the name Chicken Rock virtually wrote itself.

Ships' graveyard: Kitterland, a large rock in the Sound favoured by seals, and the tidal waters which rip through the channel and are easily capable of dragging a vessel's hull over the ragged Chicken Rock reef. Beyond is the Calf of Man.

and tied together so that you could never get to the bottom of which worm was on the end. And sure enough, once you're on this graveyard trail it's addictive – a kind of subterranean family tree hunt. You just have to keep digging.

So where does your spade lead you next? To the far north, the burial place in South Shields of one William Wouldhave – an interesting name in the circumstances, suggesting that William would have invented the lifeboat if Lionel Lukin hadn't beaten him to it. But no, William's memorial proudly and unambiguously states that it was he who blessed mankind with the invention of the lifeboat, so there. It doesn't actually add anything to the effect of "so don't believe that lying toad Lukin down there in Kent", but there is unmistakeable tension in the air, and is that the wind you can hear or the bickering of long departed souls?

And even this is not the end of the trail. You haven't yet visited the other gravestone in this epic voyage for the truth – that of one Henry Greathead. Another interesting name: maybe *he* was the real brains then. But by now you're rapidly approaching the point of past caring, in need of rescuing from your task, even when you subsequently discover that the 1789 unsinkable Greathead boat went on to achieve national fame as the Original (that's what it was called) lifeboat and Douglas acquired one in 1802. And then your interest in the story is rekindled just a tad when the name of a certain crew member of this Douglas boat leaps out and saves you from falling into a deep sleep. Sir William Hillary. The man

who didn't invent lifeboats but who first recognised the need for a national sea rescue service and provided the vision and impetus and leadership which made the foundation of the RNLI possible – an achievement for which he received a gold medal.

Getting on for two centuries down the line, the Isle of Man has five RNLI lifeboat stations. It sounds a lot for one island, but there are a hundred miles of coastline and it's pretty tricky – reefs and rocks just lying in wait, ready to bite the bum of any boat that's silly enough to venture too close or is delivered on a plate to their chomping teeth by conniving currents and evil weather. The approach to Douglas harbour is typical of the danger. Coming in on the ferry you can't miss Conister Rock, landmarked by Hillary's Tower of Refuge (for shipwrecked sailors). Unfortunately, throughout the port's maritime history, many ships have failed to miss it too, discovering to their cost that Conister is the head of a treacherous reef.

The many wrecks which have accumulated over time and now decorate the seabed around the island like arty bits of quaint rusting garden furniture are a fascination for divers – that species of human which isn't content to be merely beside the seaside but is compelled to be beside the sea creatures. And what do these creatures of the Irish Sea make of the drama and commotion of a wrecked ship sinking to a watery grave?

One of the most tragic examples – of *Titanic* proportions, and just three years after the demise of Belfast's short-lived giant itself – was the loss of

Along the top of these cliffs runs Marine Drive, connecting Douglas Head with Port Soderick. At least, it used to, before a landslide sent a large section of it crashing to the shoreline in 1977. It has never been repaired because the cost is prohibitive.

131

Right: At one time Ramsey was the centre of a thriving shipbuilding industry and other business, with tall warehouses lining the harbour. The iron swingbridge is still a prominent feature, but pleasure boats are the main attraction now.

Below right: In silhouette the Tower of Refuge and Conister Rock look like a submarine about to submerge.

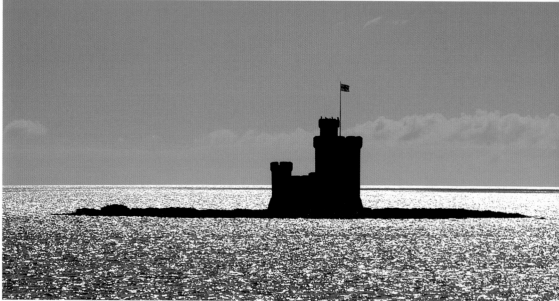

Left: **Port St Mary is the island's main sailing centre and for many years has been banging the drum and knocking on Tynwald's door for a marina development.**

Below left: **Nearby, across the narrow shoulder of the Mull Peninsula, is Port Erin and its wide, sheltered bay overlooked by Bradda Head and the unmistakeable landmark of Milner's Tower.**

133

Worn with pride

Sir William Hillary was awarded four gold medals for his services to lifeboats and saving lives at sea – one in recognition of his founding what eventually became the Royal National Lifeboat Institution, and three more for gallantry as a crew member.

He also helped establish four lifeboat stations on the Isle of Man, of which Douglas, Peel and Ramsey still survive as some of the oldest of the RNLI's current 200 or so stations.

Since 1937, all RNLI medals awarded for gallantry have borne the head of William Hillary on the obverse side.

Photo courtesy of John Stokes

the American liner *Lusitania*. On the afternoon of 7th May 1915 the four-funnelled ship, carrying almost 2,000 passengers and crew, was torpedoed off the east coast of Ireland by a German U-boat. Nearby, working in the Kinsale mackerel fishery, was the Manx fishing lugger *Wanderer*, from Peel, with seven men onboard. The skipper was William Ball of Jurby. Seeing *Lusitania* go down they headed to the scene, the first rescue boat to arrive and well ahead of any other. Some passengers and crew had made it into the water in the ship's yawls (lifeboats) and *Wanderer's* crew were able to take 140 of the 600 survivors to the safety of dry land by a combination of transferring as many as possible to the fishing boat from one yawl and then taking two other yawls in tow. For the first person they took aboard *Wanderer* – a child just two months old – this was a very eventful start to life. And it was precisely two months later, at the Isle of Man's annual Tynwald Day ceremony, when each of the Peel boat's seven heroes was presented with a medal for his actions.

High drama was also top of the menu in the astonishing story of the Christmas roast. The year was 1960, the date was 23rd December and the place was Chicken Rock, a particularly foul reef just a mile south of the Calf of Man.

What puts this maritime graveyard at the cutting edge of shipwrecking is nature's awesome combination of very deep water, the enormous power of the riptide currents racing between the Calf of Man and the Sound, and the thick sea mist which frequently hangs around in these

Left: Not all sheep are native Loaghtans, but they all graze on pastureland in typically spectacular coastal locations such as this on Maughold Head. The view is south, towards Dhoon Glen.

Below left: Looking across Douglas Bay towards the harbour and sea terminal from the promenade's Onchan (northern) end.

135

The Isle of Man is a regular port of call for luxury cruiseliners.

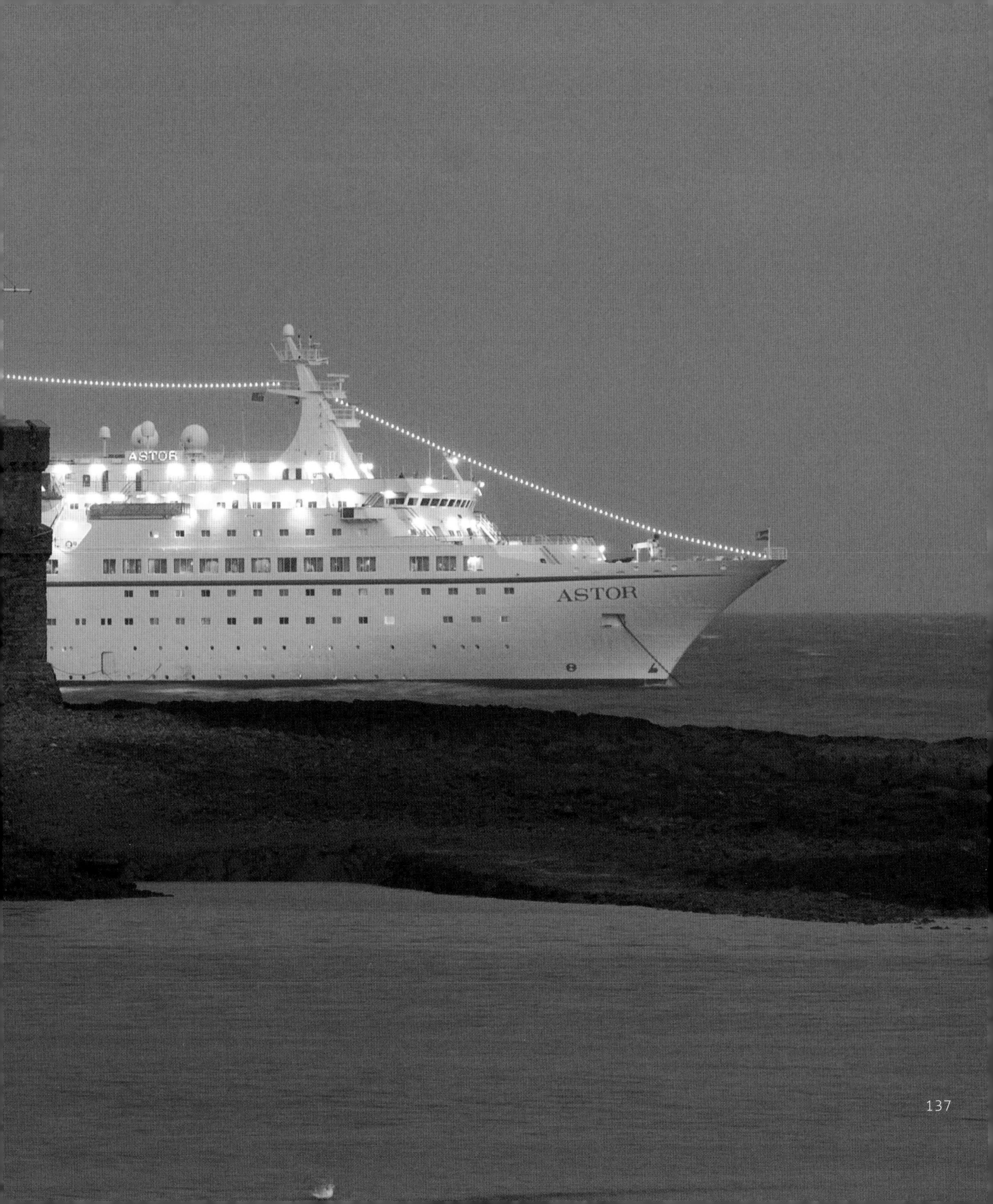
ASTOR
ASTOR

It's that incredible sea mist again, clinging to the west coast like clouds of sticky cotton wool. It's very dramatic when viewed like this from the safety of the land – but not nearly so interesting when you're out on the Irish Sea and the fog is suddenly upon you and obscuring your judgement.

parts to further fog the judgement of even the most skilled skipper. All the more amazing that in such a hostile environment, Victorian engineers managed to construct Chicken Rock lighthouse, a tower rising from the reef to a height of 144 feet (44 metres) and operational since 1st January 1875.

With Christmas Day 1960 just over the horizon, it was the lighthouse itself which made headlines around the world. The coastguard on nearby Spanish Head saw smoke coming from the tower and Port St Mary's RNLI lifeboat was despatched to the scene. To escape the fire the three duty keepers had hurriedly climbed down a rope from the uppermost room, the lantern gallery, and were standing on the rock. Their position was precarious. Having no time to don waterproof clothing they were at the mercy of the elements and the tide was rising. There was also the danger that the large fuel tanks in the lighthouse could explode at any moment. To make matters worse, the lifeboat was unable to get close enough to reach them. An RAF Air-Sea Rescue helicopter flew in from Anglesey but there was severe risk that the rotor blades could smash into the tower. So the onus was back on the lifeboat crew to use their ingenuity and effect a rescue by any means possible, or impossible if necessary. It wouldn't be the first time.

The first of the keepers was eventually taken off the rock by breeches buoy after a rope was secured to the lighthouse ladder. But he almost didn't make it, a huge wave sweeping him into the sea, luckily within reach of the crew. They were able to drag him aboard, the lifeboat then returning to Port St Mary because he needed medical attention. Eight hours after the event began, the other two stranded keepers were rescued when the receding tide and calming seas

William Milner was a safemaker from Liverpool and a generous benefactor to the poor of Port Erin. Milner's Tower was a memorial to him, built during his lifetime, in appreciation of all he did for them.

finally allowed the lifeboats of Port St Mary and Port Erin to reach them.

They were the last keepers to man Chicken Rock lighthouse on a regular basis but, contrary to many accounts, it was not abandoned in the sense of no longer being operational. The fire damage was repaired and the lighthouse continued to function as an unmanned station. It still does, having been switched to automatic operation in 1995 and now solar powered.

And it's a rescue story which highlights the great bravery of the men and women of the RNLI – not a chicken among them.

Just south of Peel is Niarbyl – a name meaning 'tail' and describing the reef. It is a quiet but very popular spot, particularly since Manx National Heritage built a visitor centre and cafe here. Niarbyl has also achieved lasting fame in *Waking Ned* and other popular films.

As the captured herring shouted defiantly, trying to wriggle out of the dock,

"Go ahead then – impose your smoking bans

– but it's not the way to cure us."

TEN

There's no smoke without kippers

Fish have their pride. And when it comes to meeting their maker, they like to feel that their lives have had some meaning. Hence this particular herring was gutted. Not for him the dignity of time-honoured chimneys and the flavouring aroma of oak and wood chips and the satisfaction of being presented proudly on a plate as a fine example of a traditional smoked kipper. Instead he was to be carted off unceremoniously to the faceless modern factory, just another piece of fish to be processed and dyed on the robotic production line. A kipper of sorts, but not the real thing. Farewell, cruel world.

The idea of smoking fresh fish and meat to preserve it is centuries old, and traditional kipper producers tend to be family businesses with a reputation established over several generations. This is true of Moore's of Peel – the last Isle of Man kippery, and still using a traditional smokehouse, with a museum and shop on site. Manx kippers are exported and enjoyed all over the world, and have been for decades.

Peel's celebrated kippers are not without competition, some of it as local as Mallaig and Argyll in Scotland and Northumberland in north-east England. The once-rich herring grounds of the Irish Sea, North Sea and Scottish lochs lend themselves to regional variations in size, colour and taste, the latter further influenced by the smoking process itself. So each producer offers kippers which in some way or other are a little bit different, special and distinctive.

Predictably, for anyone with half a mind to do so, tracing the origin of kippers is not easy,

"There's nothing fishy about these kippers – they're the genuine article!"

history as ever stubbornly refusing to serve up the required facts on a plate. However, a preliminary trawl through the annals brings up a suggestion that as long ago as 1599 somebody

143

Above: Clearing a way through the snow drifts was a job for the Army after one particularly extreme bout of bad weather left the island's roads choked and impassable.

Right: Archibald Knox (1865-1933) was an artist of great renown. Examples of his watercolours are displayed in the Manx Museum's art gallery, and he achieved commercial success with Liberty's of London, for whom he produced many English Art Nouveau designs, developing his own unique style of Celtic revival. His Scottish father, Robert, was a marine and fishing equipment engineer.

144

named Nashe wrote something about a Great Yarmouth fisherman who somehow discovered by accident that smoking herring was a good idea. *By accident?* Does this mean he accidentally made a fortune from it? If you're going to have an accident, this sounds like the sort to have.

Much more certain is that Peel has been a fishing port for centuries, as supported by the old local saying that the sea feeds more Manx people than the soil. But it was not until the 19th century that fishing truly developed into an industry, the fleet numbering more than 200 boats by the early 1880s. Any idea that they only fished a few miles or so offshore for their rich pickings is misplaced. The Irish Kinsale mackerel fishery, from which the Peel boat *Wanderer* was able to help in the *Lusitania* rescue, is over 200 miles from Peel – a voyage that under sail could take up to 30 hours. Lerwick in Shetland was another distant ground. And wherever the boats ventured, with them went the superstitions of Manx folklore, exaggerated and altered from generation to generation but still fascinating and fun to recount today – as in the following single-sentence examples.

The best safeguard against shipwreck was to ensure that you didn't leave port without a few wren feathers onboard. It was unlucky to carry sea boots on your shoulder or to place boots on the table. To ensure favourable winds, it was best to buy magic knots and tie them on a handkerchief or a belt of woven flax. After unloading a good catch and washing your boat down, it was essential to sprinkle salt all over it to

prevent evil spirits getting aboard and changing
your luck. After eating herrings you had to throw
the bones in the fire or next year the fish would
be scarce. It was very lucky to catch the first bee
you saw in April and keep it in your purse
because it was the sign of a good season. Good-
luck doctors were very fashionable, sprinkling
boat and nets with herb broth and giving a dose
of the dregs to the skipper. If you forgot to bring
something from home on a Monday morning you
should not turn back because things would go
against you all week.

After picking their way precariously through
this minefield of superstition – and the examples
above are the tip of the iceberg – it's astonishing
that the men of the Peel fleet ever found time to
do any fishing. And did harbourside Customs &
Excise actually start life as customs and exorcise?

Of all these colourful traditions, one in
particular could well have caught the fancy of
Peter Scott, the eminent English artist,
ornithologist, broadcaster and famous son of the
ill-fated Antarctic explorer Robert Falcon Scott.
Knighted in 1973, Sir Peter was a man of many
achievements, one being his appointment, in
October 1962, to the ancient and esteemed office
of Admiral of the Manx Herring Fleet at Peel. At
the time he was a Royal Navy Commander and,
given his passion for birds, it's not beyond the
bounds of possibility that he wore a wren feather
or two in his cap for good luck. If his astonishing
CV is anything to go by (post-Peel it included
founding the Wildfowl & Wetlands Trust at
Slimbridge on the Severn estuary in

Not to be outdone by Peel, Douglas has its fishing boats too.

145

Right: Peel boats are as safe as houses in the harbour, but tussling with the Irish Sea to persuade it to give up its herring shoals is not always plain sailing.

Far right: Standing outside the Standard Bank in Douglas is this lasting memorial to T.E. Brown (1830-97), the Manx national poet, who was born in the island's capital. A room in the Manx Museum is dedicated to his life and work and contains many of his manuscripts, printed works and letters.

There are no kippers without smoke

To people of a particularly sensitive disposition (and others of a questionable mentality), the knowledge that fresh fish has been cured immediately prompts the anxious questions, "Why? What disease did it have? Has the vet said it's safe to eat it?"

This distraction aside, those who really know their kippers will tell you that the secret of the taste lies in the smoking time and process and that the modern trend for dyes, chemical flavouring or a token minimal-smoking attempt bears no comparison with the traditional method.

The herring which graduate to the status of Manx kippers are fished in the months June to August, before spawning, as this is when their oil content is at its maximum. They are split, gutted, cleaned and soaked in a brine mixture before being racked for chimney smoking over oak chips, a practice dating back at this site in Peel to 1882. You can see how it's all done by joining a 40-minute tour of the Moore's kippery.

As well as the nutritional benefits they provide, oil-rich chimney-smoked kippers are (paradoxically perhaps in the light of their long tradition) a real convenience food – quick and easy to cook by boiling, grilling or microwaving.

146

Gloucestershire) this old Manx maritime superstition certainly worked for him.

The year before Scott was knighted, the Peel boats netted a record herring catch of more than 63,000 cran. Cran was one of the head-scratching words you could well have picked up on a heaving quayside or in a thriving fish market. It was a unit for measuring fresh herring, one cran being the equivalent of 37.5 gallons, or 170.5 litres – in anyone's bucket, an awful lot of fish, especially when multiplied by 63,000. Everyone on the island must have had kippers coming out of their ears for years afterwards. No wonder this was the decade in which worries over depleting fish stocks saw the introduction of measures of a different kind – those aimed at conservation. But when the weather turned bad, it was preservation (as in self) that most concerned the men of the Manx fishing fleet.

The Irish Sea can whip up a pretty hostile environment when the mood takes it, and the Isle of Man is no stranger to the odd bout of extreme weather – or even an extreme bout of extreme weather, as in the four successive years from 1929 to 1932.

The battering began with the snowstorm of '29. In some parts of the island drifts were 15 feet deep, making road and rail travel impossible. The sea was caught cold too. Had it been the herring season the fish would have been fit only for the freezer, as the ship *Peel Castle* discovered. It was en route to Liverpool from the island when frozen steering gear left it stranded for 11 hours. The vessel *Mona*, coming the other way,

Left: Evening – the perfect time for reflection in Douglas harbour.

149

Looking north to the distinctive Point of Ayre lighthouse, where the racing tidal currents are as treacherous as those at the Sound in the south. Across the water is the Scottish coastline, so near yet so far, with no connecting boat services.

Top: Jurby, an active RAF Spitfire base in the war years, now plays host to a variety of motorsport events.

Above: Pure nostalgia – but this is not the Manx Telecom phone box used by those happy Christmas pensioners!

13 Manx firsts and milestones

Next time you're in the company of people you'd really like to impress but the conversation has hit a bit of a low point, seize the opportunity to put yourself firmly in the spotlight by either
(a) showing off your expert knowledge of kippers, or
(b) asserting your tremendous talent for other Manx trivia.

- The first telephone call from the Calf of Man was made on 23rd September 1932.

- The first traffic lights were installed on the Isle of Man in 1932 – at an accident blackspot in Douglas.

- In a freak accident at Port Jack in 1934, a woman who fell over a cliff was miraculously saved – by a dead man. Her boyfriend had fallen first but she survived when she landed on top of him.

- In 1948 Douglas harbour became the first in the world to be equipped with radar.

- On 8th June 1962, Beryl Swain became the first woman to compete in a solo class of the TT when she rode in the new 50cc race.

- The first time that the helicopter ambulance airlifted an injured TT rider to hospital was on 10th June 1963.

- Manx Radio made its first ever broadcast during the 1964 TT festival.

- The first Isle of Man passports were issued on 5th July 1968.

- In 1970 the island's first drugs case was heard in court.

- In the week before the Isle of Man and Britain switched to decimal currency on 15th February 1971, banks were anxious to clear cheques written in the old currency as quickly as possible and an aircraft was chartered by the British Bankers Association solely for this purpose, flying sack loads of cheques to and from the island.

- The first Manx £10 notes were issued on 23rd June 1971.

- The Isle of Man is probably the only place in the world where a future Formula One world champion has legally driven a police car. Nigel Mansell, then a resident, joined the island's Special Constabulary in 1987.

- On 23rd December 1991, Manx Telecom wished island pensioners a merry Christmas by offering them a free 5-minute phone call to a loved one anywhere in the world.

fared even worse, taking 26 agonising hours to reach Douglas. And when the snow on the island finally relented, frost took its place and the livestock of many Manx farms was decimated.

The following year brought the worst floods for a century, Laxey being the chief recipient of the resulting devastation as hurricane-force winds and intense rain ripped through walls and bridges, leaving mud and rubble in their wake and chucking in a few landslides for bad measure.

So could 1931 offer any relief? It started badly, new year fog descending on Merseyside and leaving the Isle of Man without any incoming mail or English newspapers for four days. Thick fog struck again months later, ten lives lost when a steamer sank after hitting rocks near Port Erin. And the first earthquake to rumble the island for more than a hundred years provided further shocks – as did the death of Sir Hall Caine, Manx novelist and playwright, at the age of 78 on the last day of August.

August 1932 was also a bad month, the weather baring its fangs with a vengeance as an incredible six-hour rainstorm put a damper on holiday fun and flooded Douglas promenade. And the terrible Thirties continued to wreak havoc in this decade of destruction, bringing heavy floods in 1936 and blizzards in 1937.

Yet, offered the choice, everyone on the Isle of Man would have willingly suffered these setbacks in preference to the horrors of the storm which was looming ever larger on the horizon: the Second World War.

153

Geographically speaking, except for the barely discernible drift of the tectonic plate on which it stands, the Isle of Man is exactly where it was in the mid 19th century, when those Victorian holidaymakers started to arrive – but the world has moved on a lot since then. Or has it?

ELEVEN

We do like to do it beside the seaside

Bizarrely, the war proved to be a good time for the Isle of Man, economically speaking. In June 1945, just six weeks after VE Day, Tynwald's last wartime budget revealed that the island was in its strongest financial position ever.

And then there was the other surprising phenomenon (or so it seems now, but it may have been predicted or even expected then) – the holiday rush. June and July 1945 greeted the arrival of about 100,000 visitors, desperate for a break after all the horrors and hardships of six bloody war years.

But was this necessarily good news for all those businesses which pre-war represented the island's holiday industry? No! The social infrastructure was not exactly ship shape and Bristol fashion. Just about everything was in short supply, and boarding house and hotel accommodation, seconded in the war for service personnel and much of it still under this kind of military occupation, was in a shocking state and in need of repair and restoration. The problems can be gauged by the experience of one hotelier in Douglas whose 'guests' had already departed, taking his entire hotel lift system with them! That must have been some suitcase. And even allowing for the inevitable ups and downs of war, he was understandably furious at being shafted.

Further immediate post-war holiday havoc was caused by rationing and other shortages, including Steam Packet vessels. In these circumstances a boom was the last thing anybody wanted – especially of the type threatened in 1946 when sea mines were swept ashore around the island's coastline. Most were defused by Royal Navy experts but that didn't stop the price of pre-war cars going sky high. And the island's butchers let it be known that they'd welcome freshly-caught rabbits (at the same time making it abundantly clear that any quips about Hare Hitler would be regarded as in extremely bad taste).

Despite all the minor irritations and inconvenience, holidaymakers continued to invade the Isle of Man, determined to have a good time come what may. If the war had gone the other way, things could have been very different. The discovery in 1944 of the German invasion plan of Britain revealed that the island was in the direct path of the attack, had it ever happened. And how ironic that the major TV drama series *Island At War*, based on the Nazi occupation of Jersey, was shot in part in Isle of Man locations, notably Castletown. Had you casually predicted any such thing over half a pint in a Castletown pub in 1946, you'd have been carted off to a small dark room in the depths of Castle Rushen and confined to a straitjacket. Either that or put in charge of tourism.

If the latter sounds the more attractive proposition, think again. With one victory over a European foe in the bag, the Isle of Man suddenly came up against another. In 1954 a Spanish magician named Sam Costa pulled off a very cheap trick. You could go into any travel agent and over the counter buy yourself a little package which, when unwrapped, revealed a Spanish beach, fourteen days of sunshine, a room in a block of flats which was actually a brand new

The show you can take anywhere, and with timeless appeal. But somehow, so much more enjoyable when you're holidaying beside the the seaside.

155

hotel with all mod cons, and as many plane seats as you needed to fly you and the family there and back. Plus some silly hats and a stuffed donkey. This was offered in the belief that the Mediterranean was a more alluring and altogether warmer place to visit than the Irish Sea. Preposterous! Who did you think you were kidding, Mr Costa?

Only five minutes later, or so it seemed, 1979 was looming – a big, big year for the Isle of Man. The Tynwald Millennium. A thousand years of unbroken parliament (give or take the odd chair or two damaged in scuffles during the most heated debates). It would be a momentous occasion, celebrated with pomp, ceremony and style, and guaranteed to attract big numbers as well as bigwigs, notably the Queen, Prince Philip and King Olav of Norway, who was keen to renew the Isle of Man's old Norse connections.

July 5th was the big day. No King Olav. Word came through that his royal yacht *Norge* had broken down but, determined that he would not disappoint his hosts, he had valiantly transferred to the dinghy – a 6-ton, 50-foot replica Viking longship called *Odin's Raven* – which he intended to row the rest of the way single handed and expected to be there about tea time, save him a muffin. When he finally pulled into Peel, with all the dignity that befits a monarch and not a damp armpit to behold, it was August and everybody had forgotten he was coming. Asked by the local press to describe his gruelling one-man voyage, he said, simply, "Oarsome."

A few years later the Isle of Man had decided

Far left: Karting at Jurby? Or testing another secret (high-speed) moon buggy?

Top left: "You realise that if we do all nine courses we'll have another 161 holes to play after this one?"

Middle left: "Once I'm down this wall they won't realise I'm not in my bedroom."

Bottom left: "Well if this is the racecourse it seems a bit overgrown."

157

It was a different world then

- 1912: a government proposal to allow mixed bathing (male and female on the same beach) was rejected.

- 1915: the menace of German submarines was a big blow to the island's holiday trade.

- 1924: a trawler was arrested in Manx waters. Handcuffs were obviously a lot bigger in those days.

- 1932: government expenditure for the coming year was estimated at £386,500 – about the price of a new 1-bed apartment in 2008 Douglas. And in 1946 it cost £166,500 to build 110 new council houses.

- 1932: a councillor was fined 5 shillings (25 pence) for selling chocolate eclairs in his cafe on a Sunday.

- 1937: Manx Constabulary received its first 2 police cars, followed in 1938 by a CID department.

- 1947: a vicar defrocked for bigamy received 18 months' hard labour.

- 1950: parking on any of Douglas's main roads or streets was banned after the council announced that "Streets were never made for the parking of motor cars."

- 1955: a 3-month sentence for a woman gaoled for murder.

- 1959: a byelaw made it an offence to smoke or play cards in taxis. And although a bill to legalise football pools betting failed, a Peel family won a £750,000 pools jackpot in 1985.

and it's a different world now

- 1980: Ramsey man found guilty of growing cannabis in a record player.

- 1981: census revealed that only 53% of the population was Manx born.

- 1981: traditional Manx punishment – birching – condemned by International Court of Human Rights in Strasbourg.

- 1987: amazing growth and development of finance sector.

- 1987: Manx Telecom laid a 56-mile fibre optic cable to Cumbria incorporating 8,000 simultaneous speech circuits – compared with 132 separate lines of an old cable to Colwyn Bay.

- 1991: census revealed that new residents outnumber Manx natives.

- 1996: the launch of the island's film industry, 67 years after talking films were first shown in Manx cinemas.

- 1999: breath tests for motorists introduced.

- 2000: revealed that tourism contributes only 5% of national income but is a very important employer.

- 2004: first Isle of Man walking festival.

Top: This internment camp at Ramsey was one of several which during the Second World War were home to 14,000 aliens – not one of whom was green or had antennae but would probably have given anything to phone home!

Bottom left: More than 60 years on, the commercial heart of Douglas's thriving banking and financial centre – Athol Street and Prospect Hill.

Bottom right: Pre-dating both: exploring the Isle of Man by charabanc was a real adventure in the 1920s. This new-fangled mode of transport could cover more miles in a day than horsedrawn vehicles and encouraged the Steam Packet to run five Round the Island sailings a week.

that future prosperity lay in promoting the island as an attractive low-tax offshore financial centre – quite a change from a traditional bucket-and-spade holiday destination, though cleverly one proposition didn't negate the other. And anyway, it didn't matter because a new generation of visitors had discovered other good reasons for making regular trips across the Irish Sea.

There were those little holes in the ground, for instance – lots of them, and by an amazing coincidence the ideal size for golf balls. And the trails and tracks and footpaths that led to extraordinary and beautiful places. And annual events and festivals and other enchantments which had been there along but were suddenly more noticeable because of renewed Manx pride and interest in making them known to the wider world. Communication was all the rage.

One of the biggest challenges and innovations, and by definition a never-ending story, was and is the all-out effort to promote the surprising number of aspects of the island's history, heritage and culture – but in ways that wouldn't and won't entice those people who don't have a natural curiosity for things past to launch themselves from the top of the Laxey wheel or eat their own heads, or each other, out of boredom.

This emphasis on the island's heritage has been up and running since 1986 and to date there have been no reported incidents of such leaps or acts of cannibalism, so it's fairly safe to assume that there haven't been any. The Manx police and media are pretty hot on this sort of thing.

Top left: If Isle of Man ferries went as fast as powerboats you could combine flying and sailing in the same trip!

Top right: "Seriously, Dad, this bathroom's flooded!"
Or maybe it's the boating lake in Ramsey's Mooragh Park.

Bottom left: Andreas in the north was an active wartime Spitfire base, and here's a modern-day quadron preparing to take off.

Bottom right: "Steady, love – I think you've dropped one." There are enough greens on the Isle of Man to bowl any fan over.

"I'm sure I dropped those car keys *somewhere* round here."

162

Top right: "I'd like two pairs of shoes for my horse, please. Size sixteen hands." The blacksmith's shop at Cregneash.

Middle right: "How come they never do this at Ronaldsway!" A spectacular Jurby air show.

Bottom right: *Odin's Raven* – the replica longship which King Olav left in the House of Manannan in 1979. Which was quite a trick considering that this Peel heritage attraction wasn't built and didn't open until 1996.

Far right: Escaping from Alcatraz. Al Capone is the one in the middle. On the other hand, it could be kayakers with a passion for doing it beside the seaside – in this case just off St Patrick's Isle, Peel.

In fact, the opposite is true. Awards have been won (prestigious and independent awards at that, given in the name of imaginative and interesting presentation), pinned to the lapels of both the Manx Museum and the House of Manannan. It goes without saying that the aforementioned pins have no sharp bits, edges or appendages, or in any way pose a danger, as health and safety laws absolutely forbid it.

On the subject of obsessions, it could be argued that tourism in the 21st century, virtually everywhere on the globe, is based on the massive assumption that you have to provide your visitors with lots of things to do. Busy busy busy. But hold on there a moment: isn't the idea of a holiday the same as it's always been? To relax? Take it easy? Let go? Do nothing? Recharge your batteries? In fact, isn't this particularly true since we all work longer hours, live more complicated and stressful lives, and perform more juggling tricks in a week than a three-legged circus maestro could cope with in a lifetime?

The Isle of Man gives you the choice. All day long you can walk, cycle, ride, climb, dive, sail, swim, fish, bowl and hit as many golf balls as you like. Or you can treat every day as a Good Friday bank holiday and be as free as Robinson Crusoe.

Doctor Russell was crazy enough to advocate drinking sea water, but many people today will agree that he was right about one thing. Whatever you decide to do, and however many legs you happen to have, there's nothing quite as invigorating – and nothing better for health and wellbeing – than doing it beside the seaside.

Acknowledgements

Lily Publications are grateful to everyone who has helped in the creation of this book, including the use of additional photographs, and apologise for any names inadvertently omitted from this alphabetical listing.

Helena Axon of Visit Blackpool, Stan Basnett, Mick Duckworth, Ferry Publications, Isle of Man Department of Tourism & Leisure, Andrew Lowe, Margaret McGee of Manx Telecom, the Royal National Lifeboat Institution, Roger Sims of Manx National Heritage, Bill Snelling and John Stokes.

Photographs reproduced by kind permission of Manx National Heritage are on pages 9, 10, 11, 41, 69, 116, 127, 144 and 158.

ISBN: 97818996020302

A CIP catalogue record for this book is available from the British Library.

© 2008 Lily Publications Ltd

Manx Telecom's headquarters at Braddan.

167